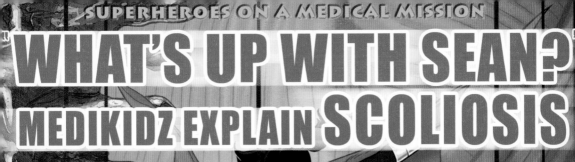

SUPERHEROES ON A MEDICAL MISSION

"WHAT'S UP WITH SEAN?"

MEDIKIDZ EXPLAIN SCOLIOSIS

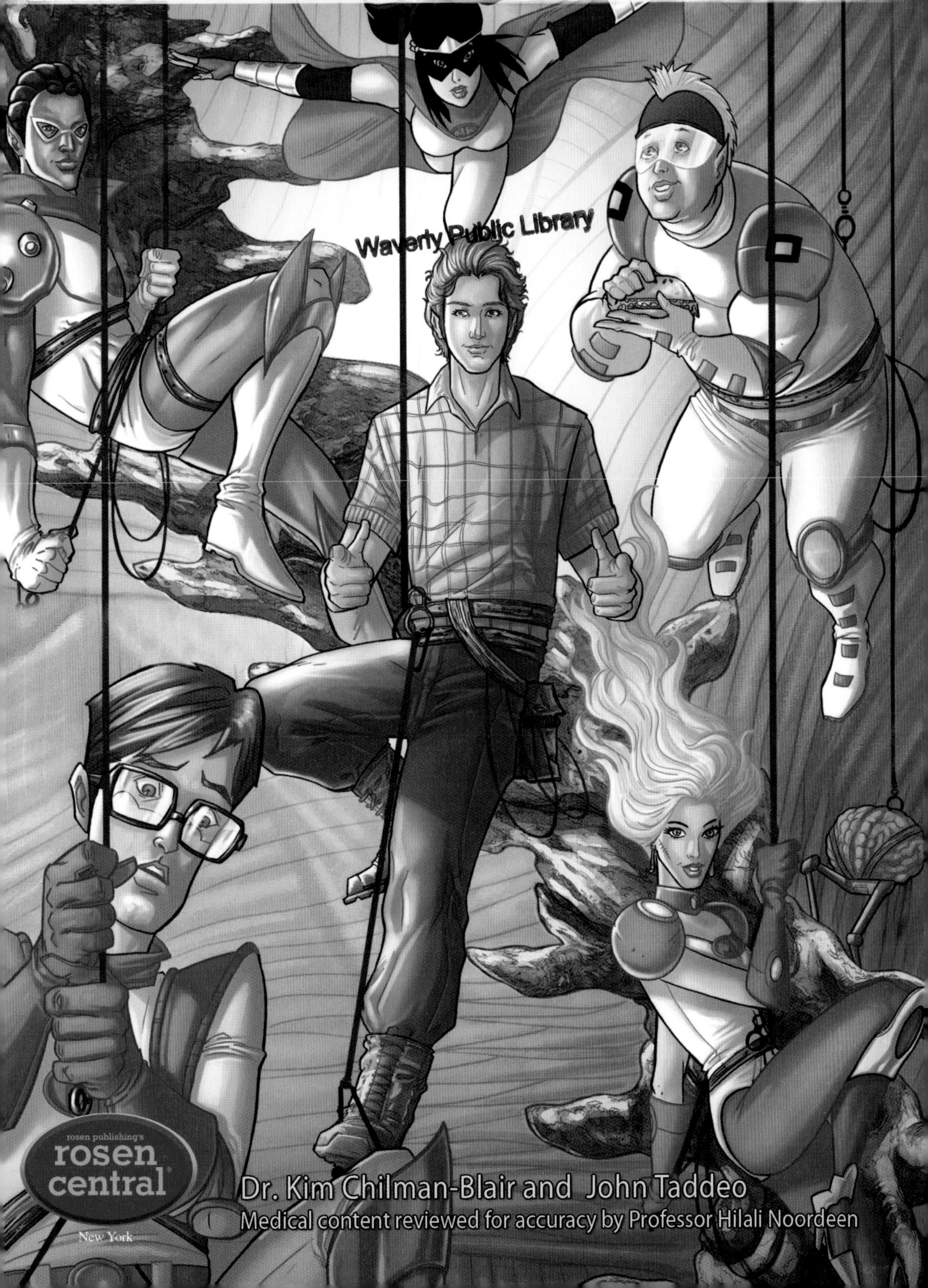

Dr. Kim Chilman-Blair and John Taddeo

Medical content reviewed for accuracy by Professor Hilali Noordeen

rosen publishing's rosen central®

New York

This edition published in 2010 by:

The Rosen Publishing Group, Inc.
29 East 21st Street
New York, NY 10010

Library of Congress Cataloging-in-Publication Data

Chilman-Blair, Dr. Kim.
"What's up with Sean?" medikidz explain scoliosis / Dr. Kim Chilman-Blair and John Taddeo; medical content reviewed for accuracy by Hilali Noordeen.
        p. cm.—(Superheroes on a medical mission)
Includes index.
ISBN 978-1-4358-3536-8 (library binding)
1. Scoliosis—Comic books, strips, etc. I. Taddeo, John. II. Noordeen, Hilali. III. Title.
RD771.S3C55 2010
616.7'3—dc22

                                                                        2009026741

Manufactured in China

CPSIA Compliance Information: Batch #MW0102YA: For Further Information contact Rosen Publishing, New York, New York at 1-800-237-9932

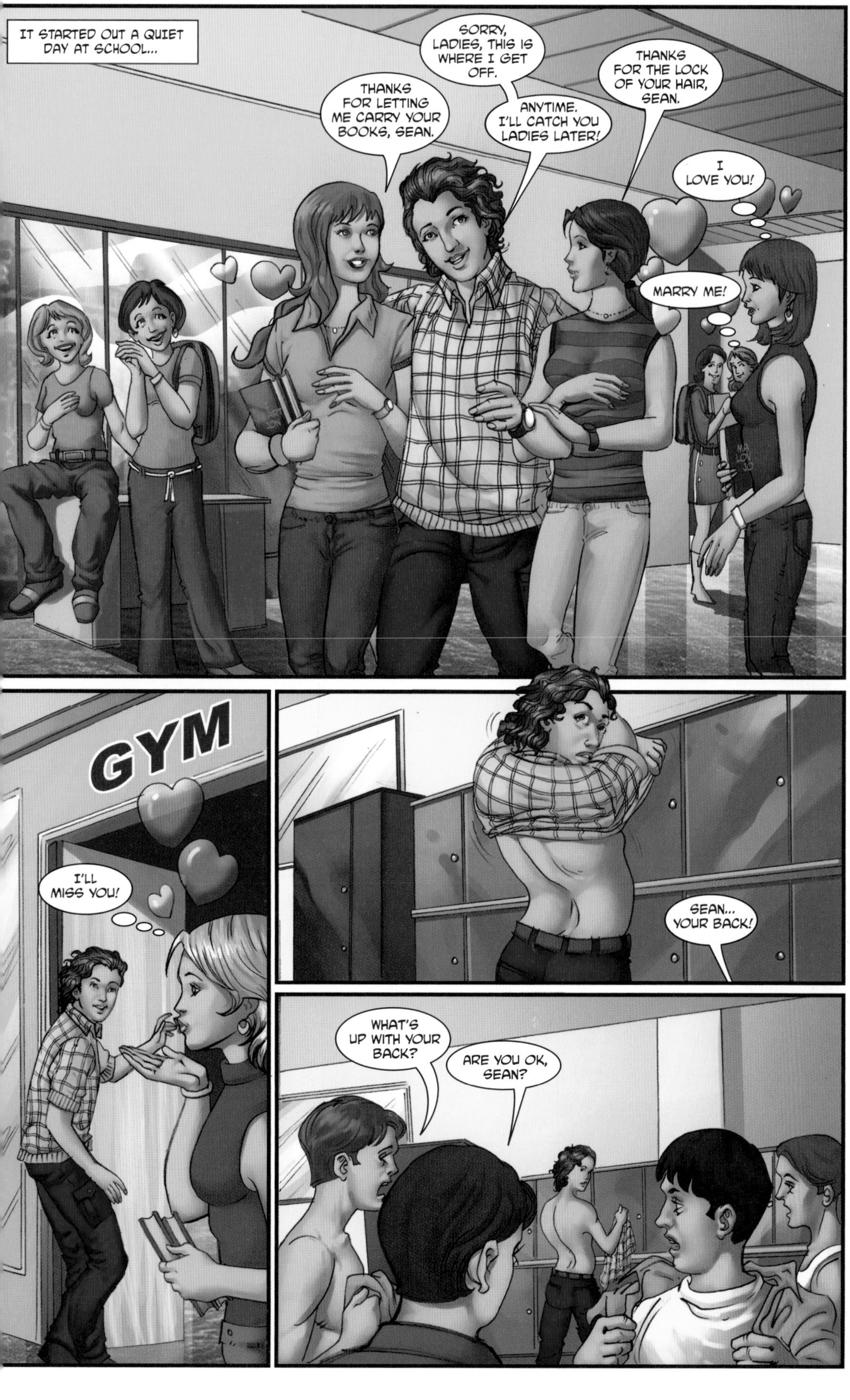
IT STARTED OUT A QUIET DAY AT SCHOOL...
THANKS FOR LETTING ME CARRY YOUR BOOKS, SEAN.
SORRY, LADIES, THIS IS WHERE I GET OFF.
ANYTIME. I'LL CATCH YOU LADIES LATER!
THANKS FOR THE LOCK OF YOUR HAIR, SEAN.
I LOVE YOU!
MARRY ME!
GYM
I'LL MISS YOU!
SEAN... YOUR BACK!
WHAT'S UP WITH YOUR BACK?
ARE YOU OK, SEAN?

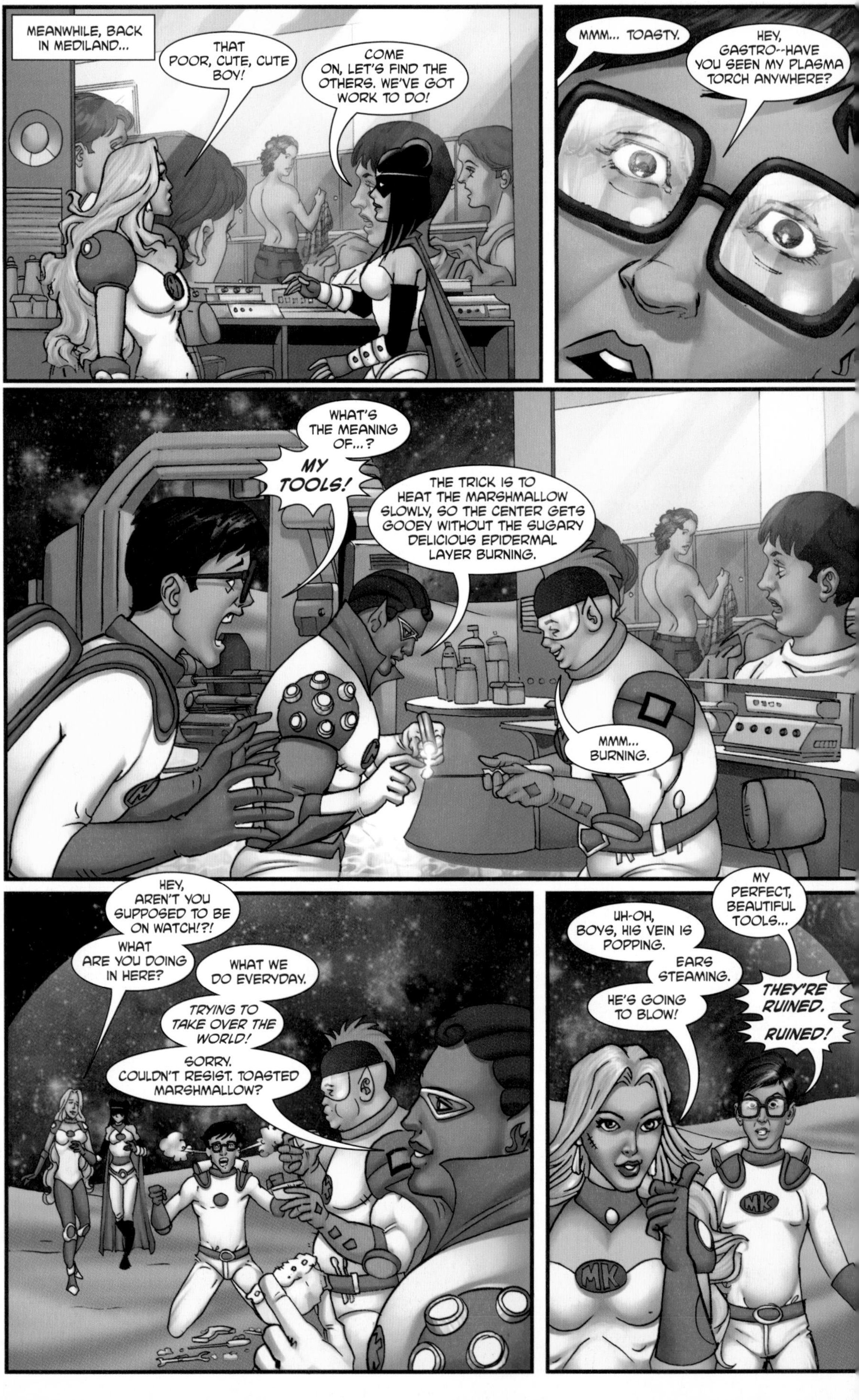

MEANWHILE, BACK IN MEDILAND...
THAT POOR, CUTE, CUTE BOY!
COME ON, LET'S FIND THE OTHERS. WE'VE GOT WORK TO DO!
MMM... TOASTY.
HEY, GASTRO--HAVE YOU SEEN MY PLASMA TORCH ANYWHERE?
WHAT'S THE MEANING OF...?
MY TOOLS!
THE TRICK IS TO HEAT THE MARSHMALLOW SLOWLY, SO THE CENTER GETS GOOEY WITHOUT THE SUGARY DELICIOUS EPIDERMAL LAYER BURNING.
MMM... BURNING.
HEY, AREN'T YOU SUPPOSED TO BE ON WATCH!?!
WHAT ARE YOU DOING IN HERE?
WHAT WE DO EVERYDAY.
TRYING TO TAKE OVER THE WORLD!
SORRY. COULDN'T RESIST. TOASTED MARSHMALLOW?
UH-OH, BOYS, HIS VEIN IS POPPING.
EARS STEAMING.
HE'S GOING TO BLOW!
MY PERFECT, BEAUTIFUL TOOLS...
THEY'RE RUINED.
RUINED!

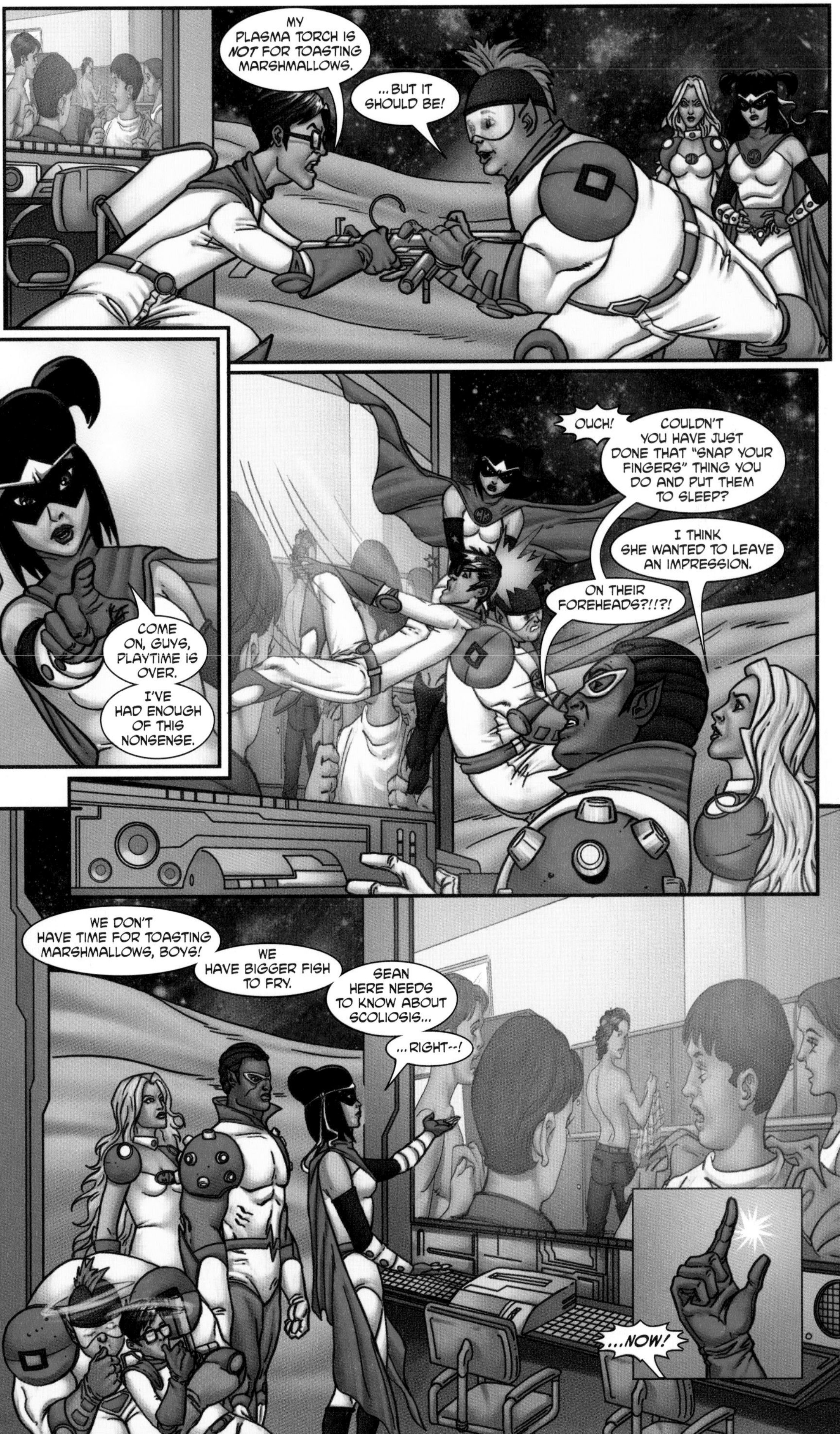
MY PLASMA TORCH IS *NOT* FOR TOASTING MARSHMALLOWS.
...BUT IT SHOULD BE!
COME ON, GUYS, PLAYTIME IS OVER.
I'VE HAD ENOUGH OF THIS NONSENSE.
OUCH!
COULDN'T YOU HAVE JUST DONE THAT "SNAP YOUR FINGERS" THING YOU DO AND PUT THEM TO SLEEP?
I THINK SHE WANTED TO LEAVE AN IMPRESSION.
ON THEIR FOREHEADS?!!?!
WE DON'T HAVE TIME FOR TOASTING MARSHMALLOWS, BOYS!
WE HAVE BIGGER FISH TO FRY.
SEAN HERE NEEDS TO KNOW ABOUT SCOLIOSIS...
...RIGHT--!
...NOW!

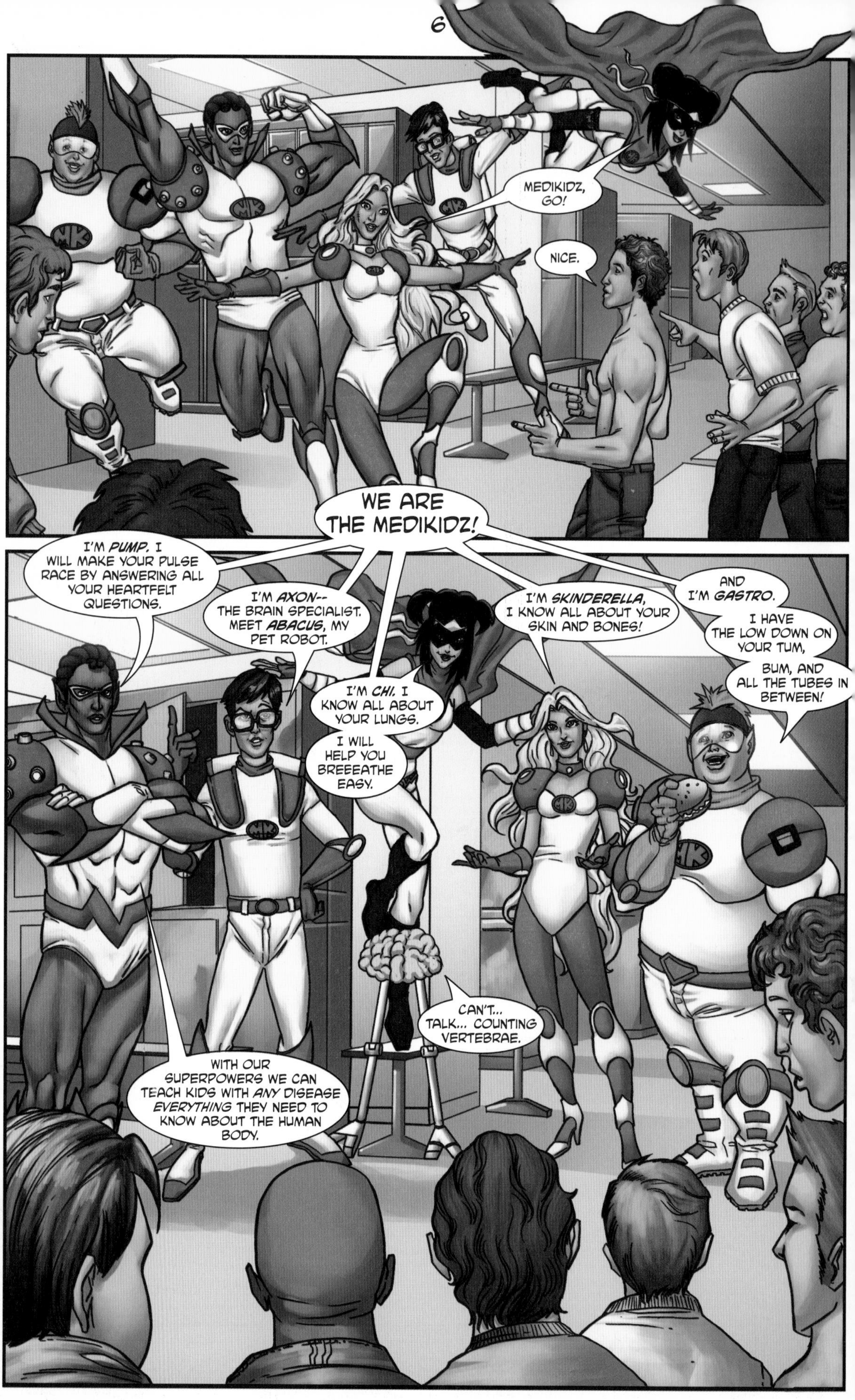
MEDIKIDZ, GO!
NICE.
WE ARE THE MEDIKIDZ!
I'M *PUMP*. I WILL MAKE YOUR PULSE RACE BY ANSWERING ALL YOUR HEARTFELT QUESTIONS.
I'M *AXON*-- THE BRAIN SPECIALIST. MEET *ABACUS*, MY PET ROBOT.
I'M *CHI*. I KNOW ALL ABOUT YOUR LUNGS.
I WILL HELP YOU BREEEATHE EASY.
I'M *SKINDERELLA*, I KNOW ALL ABOUT YOUR SKIN AND BONES!
AND I'M *GASTRO*.
I HAVE THE LOW DOWN ON YOUR TUM,
BUM, AND ALL THE TUBES IN BETWEEN!
CAN'T... TALK... COUNTING VERTEBRAE.
WITH OUR SUPERPOWERS WE CAN TEACH KIDS WITH *ANY DISEASE* *EVERYTHING* THEY NEED TO KNOW ABOUT THE HUMAN BODY.

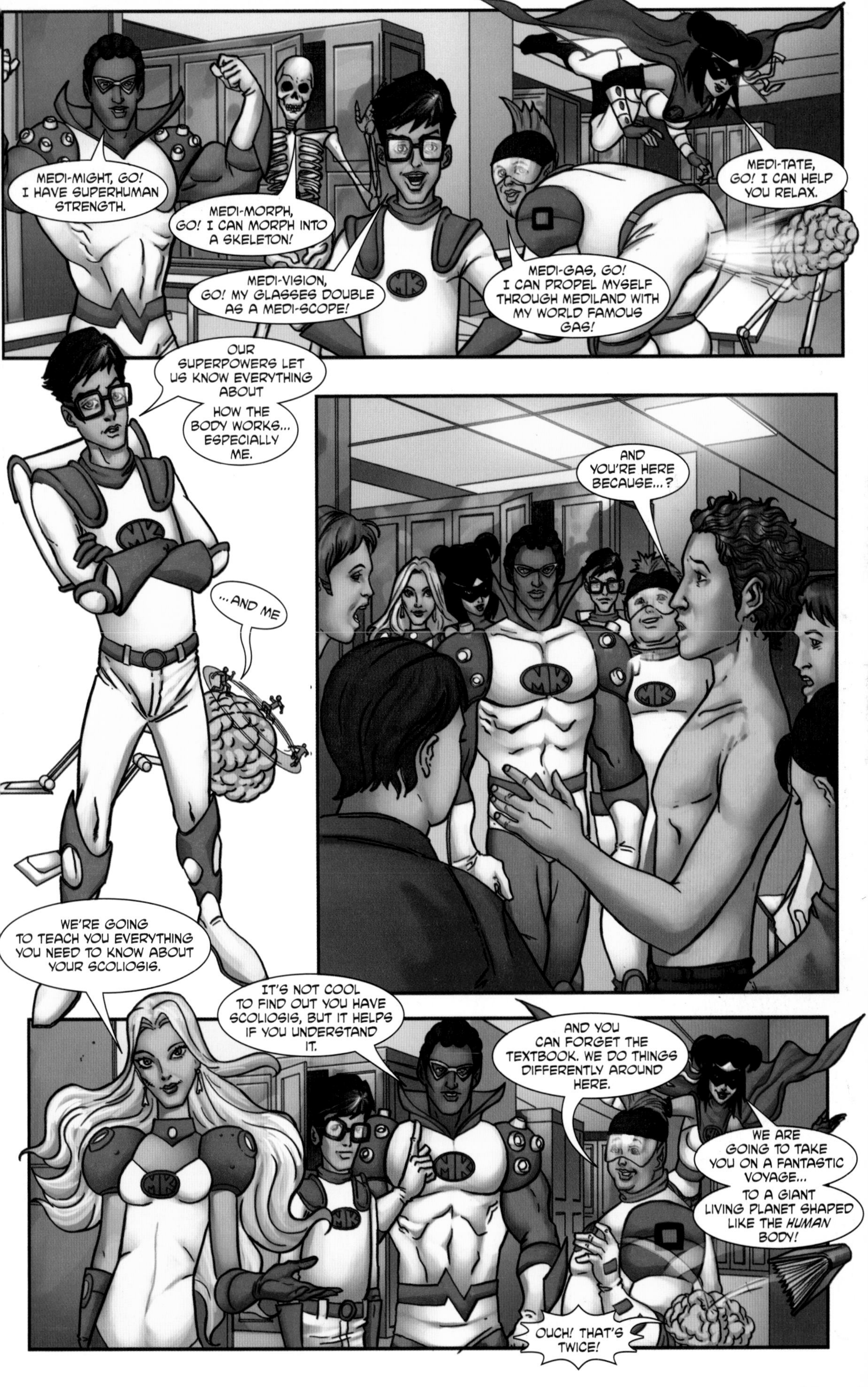
MEDI-MIGHT, GO! I HAVE SUPERHUMAN STRENGTH.
MEDI-MORPH, GO! I CAN MORPH INTO A SKELETON!
MEDI-VISION, GO! MY GLASSES DOUBLE AS A MEDI-SCOPE!
MEDI-GAS, GO! I CAN PROPEL MYSELF THROUGH MEDILAND WITH MY WORLD FAMOUS GAS!
MEDI-TATE, GO! I CAN HELP YOU RELAX.
OUR SUPERPOWERS LET US KNOW EVERYTHING ABOUT
HOW THE BODY WORKS... ESPECIALLY ME.
...AND ME
AND YOU'RE HERE BECAUSE...?
WE'RE GOING TO TEACH YOU EVERYTHING YOU NEED TO KNOW ABOUT YOUR SCOLIOSIS.
IT'S NOT COOL TO FIND OUT YOU HAVE SCOLIOSIS, BUT IT HELPS IF YOU UNDERSTAND IT.
AND YOU CAN FORGET THE TEXTBOOK. WE DO THINGS DIFFERENTLY AROUND HERE.
WE ARE GOING TO TAKE YOU ON A FANTASTIC VOYAGE...
TO A GIANT LIVING PLANET SHAPED LIKE THE *HUMAN* BODY!
OUCH! THAT'S TWICE!

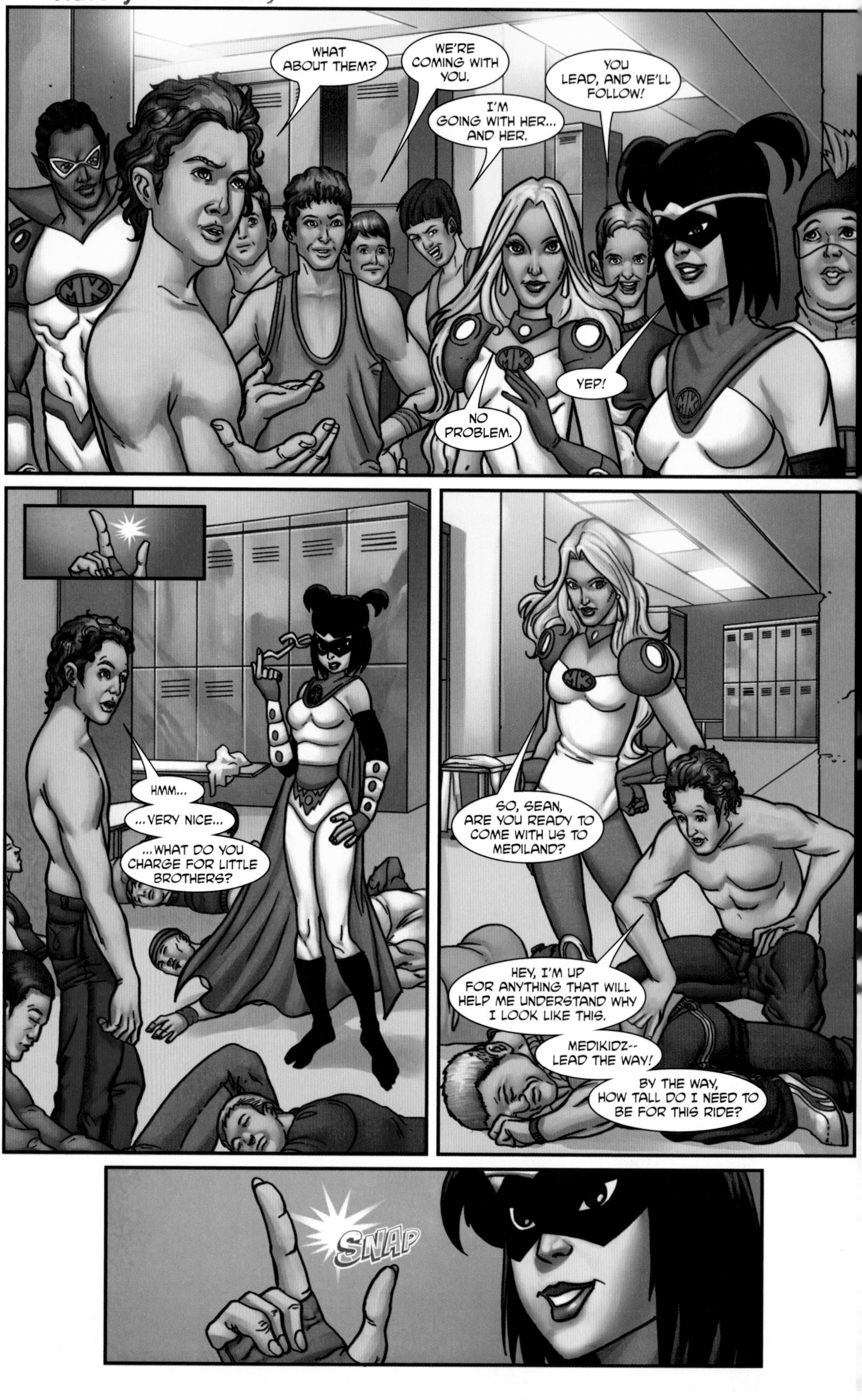
WHAT ABOUT THEM?
WE'RE COMING WITH YOU.
I'M GOING WITH HER... AND HER.
YOU LEAD, AND WE'LL FOLLOW!
NO PROBLEM.
YEP!
HMM...
...VERY NICE...
...WHAT DO YOU CHARGE FOR LITTLE BROTHERS?
SO, SEAN, ARE YOU READY TO COME WITH US TO MEDILAND?
HEY, I'M UP FOR ANYTHING THAT WILL HELP ME UNDERSTAND WHY I LOOK LIKE THIS.
MEDIKIDZ-- LEAD THE WAY!
BY THE WAY, HOW TALL DO I NEED TO BE FOR THIS RIDE?
SNAP

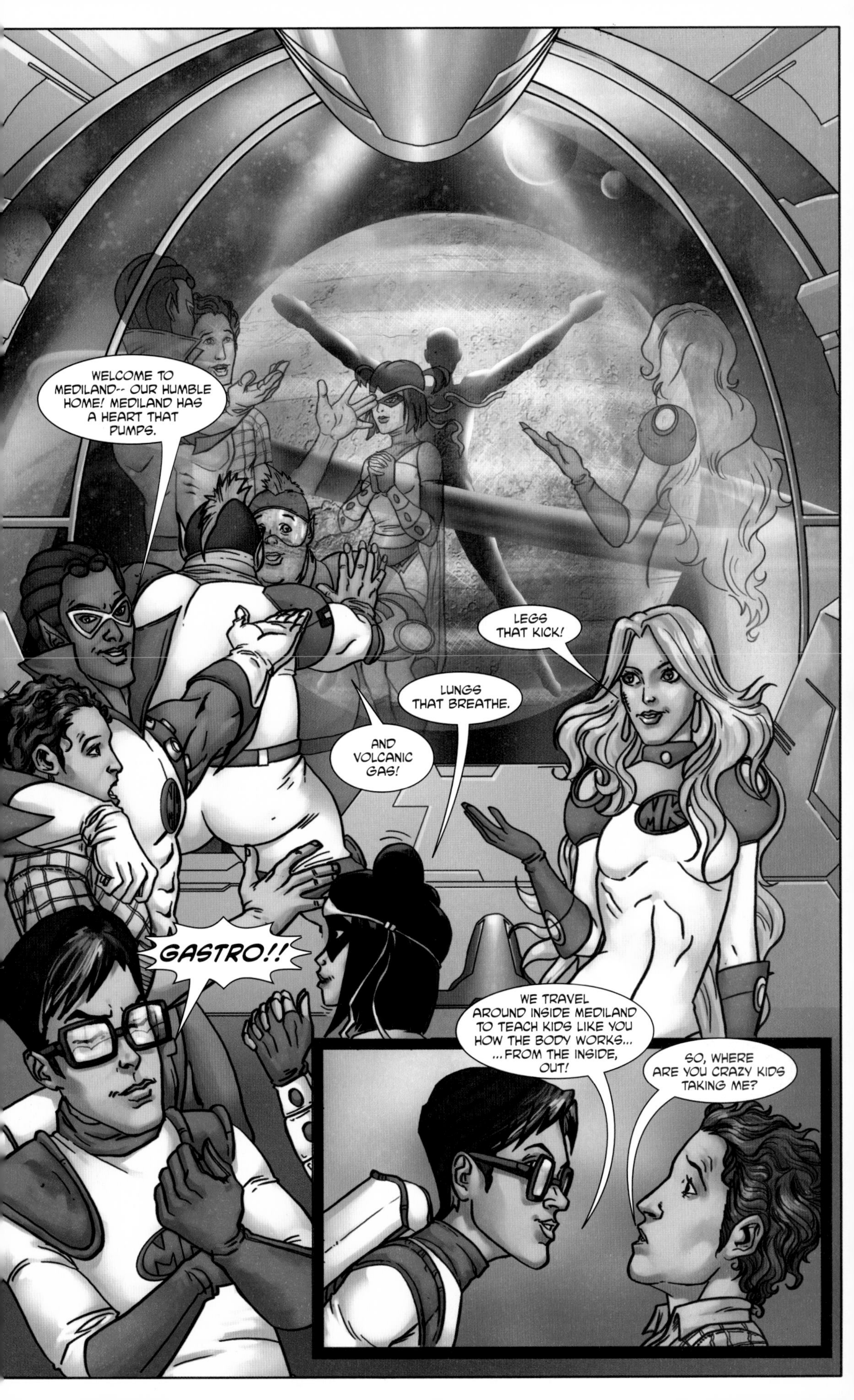
WELCOME TO MEDILAND-- OUR HUMBLE HOME! MEDILAND HAS A HEART THAT PUMPS.
LEGS THAT KICK!
LUNGS THAT BREATHE.
AND VOLCANIC GAS!
GASTRO!!
WE TRAVEL AROUND INSIDE MEDILAND TO TEACH KIDS LIKE YOU HOW THE BODY WORKS... ...FROM THE INSIDE, OUT!
SO, WHERE ARE YOU CRAZY KIDS TAKING ME?

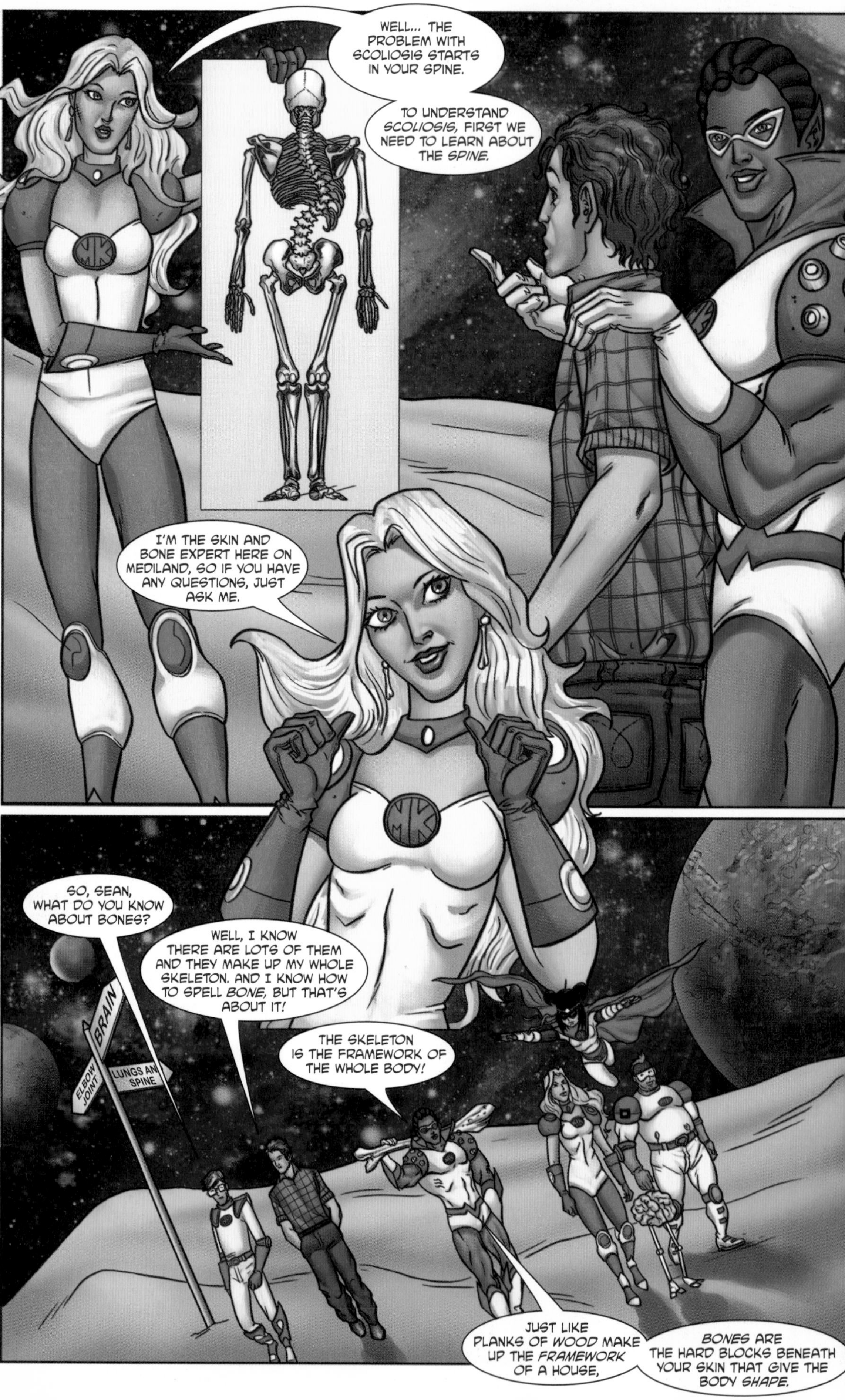
WELL... THE PROBLEM WITH SCOLIOSIS STARTS IN YOUR SPINE.
TO UNDERSTAND *SCOLIOSIS*, FIRST WE NEED TO LEARN ABOUT THE *SPINE*.
I'M THE SKIN AND BONE EXPERT HERE ON MEDILAND, SO IF YOU HAVE ANY QUESTIONS, JUST ASK ME.
SO, SEAN, WHAT DO YOU KNOW ABOUT BONES?
WELL, I KNOW THERE ARE LOTS OF THEM AND THEY MAKE UP MY WHOLE SKELETON. AND I KNOW HOW TO SPELL *BONE*, BUT THAT'S ABOUT IT!
BRAIN
ELBOW JOINT
LUNGS AN SPINE
THE SKELETON IS THE FRAMEWORK OF THE WHOLE BODY!
JUST LIKE PLANKS OF *WOOD* MAKE UP THE *FRAMEWORK* OF A HOUSE,
BONES ARE THE HARD BLOCKS BENEATH YOUR SKIN THAT GIVE THE BODY *SHAPE*.

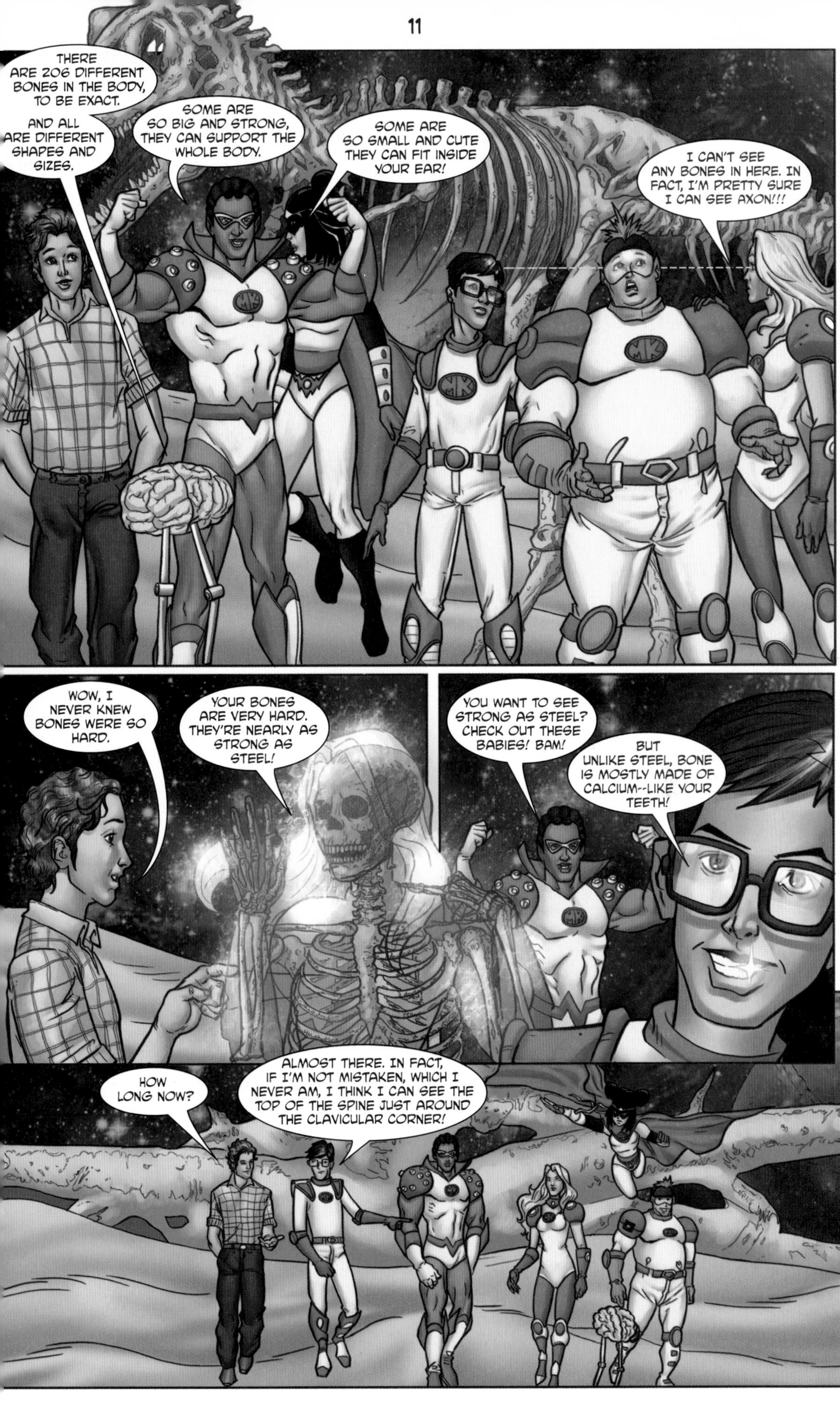
THERE ARE 206 DIFFERENT BONES IN THE BODY, TO BE EXACT.
AND ALL ARE DIFFERENT SHAPES AND SIZES.
SOME ARE SO BIG AND STRONG, THEY CAN SUPPORT THE WHOLE BODY.
SOME ARE SO SMALL AND CUTE THEY CAN FIT INSIDE YOUR EAR!
I CAN'T SEE ANY BONES IN HERE. IN FACT, I'M PRETTY SURE I CAN SEE AXON!!!
WOW, I NEVER KNEW BONES WERE SO HARD.
YOUR BONES ARE VERY HARD. THEY'RE NEARLY AS STRONG AS STEEL!
YOU WANT TO SEE STRONG AS STEEL? CHECK OUT THESE BABIES! BAM!
BUT UNLIKE STEEL, BONE IS MOSTLY MADE OF CALCIUM--LIKE YOUR TEETH!
HOW LONG NOW?
ALMOST THERE. IN FACT, IF I'M NOT MISTAKEN, WHICH I NEVER AM, I THINK I CAN SEE THE TOP OF THE SPINE JUST AROUND THE CLAVICULAR CORNER!

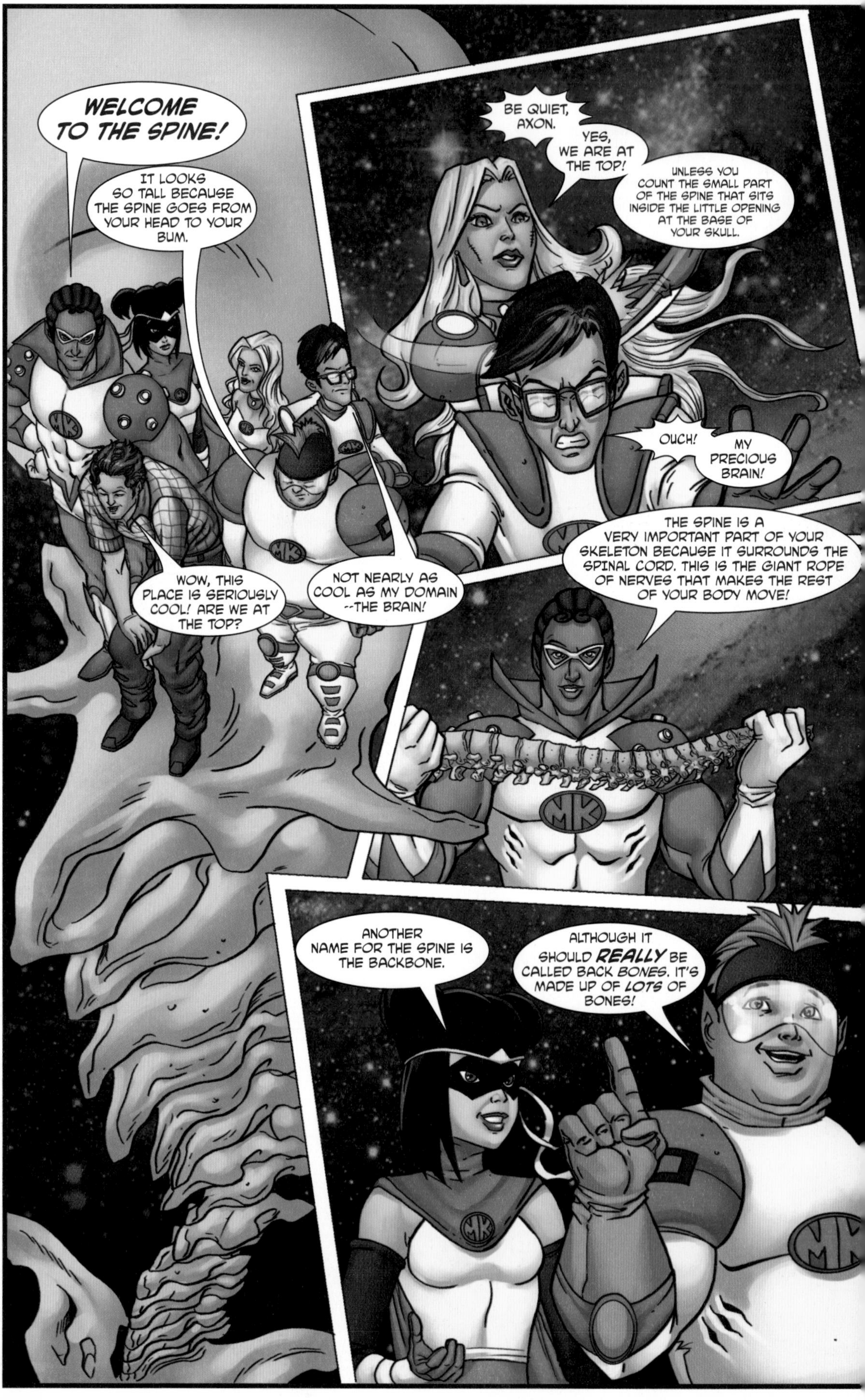
WELCOME TO THE SPINE!
IT LOOKS SO TALL BECAUSE THE SPINE GOES FROM YOUR HEAD TO YOUR BUM.
WOW, THIS PLACE IS SERIOUSLY COOL! ARE WE AT THE TOP?
NOT NEARLY AS COOL AS MY DOMAIN --THE BRAIN!
BE QUIET, AXON.
YES, WE ARE AT THE TOP!
UNLESS YOU COUNT THE SMALL PART OF THE SPINE THAT SITS INSIDE THE LITTLE OPENING AT THE BASE OF YOUR SKULL.
OUCH!
MY PRECIOUS BRAIN!
THE SPINE IS A VERY IMPORTANT PART OF YOUR SKELETON BECAUSE IT SURROUNDS THE SPINAL CORD. THIS IS THE GIANT ROPE OF NERVES THAT MAKES THE REST OF YOUR BODY MOVE!
ANOTHER NAME FOR THE SPINE IS THE BACKBONE.
ALTHOUGH IT SHOULD ***REALLY*** BE CALLED BACK *BONES*. IT'S MADE UP OF *LOTS* OF BONES!

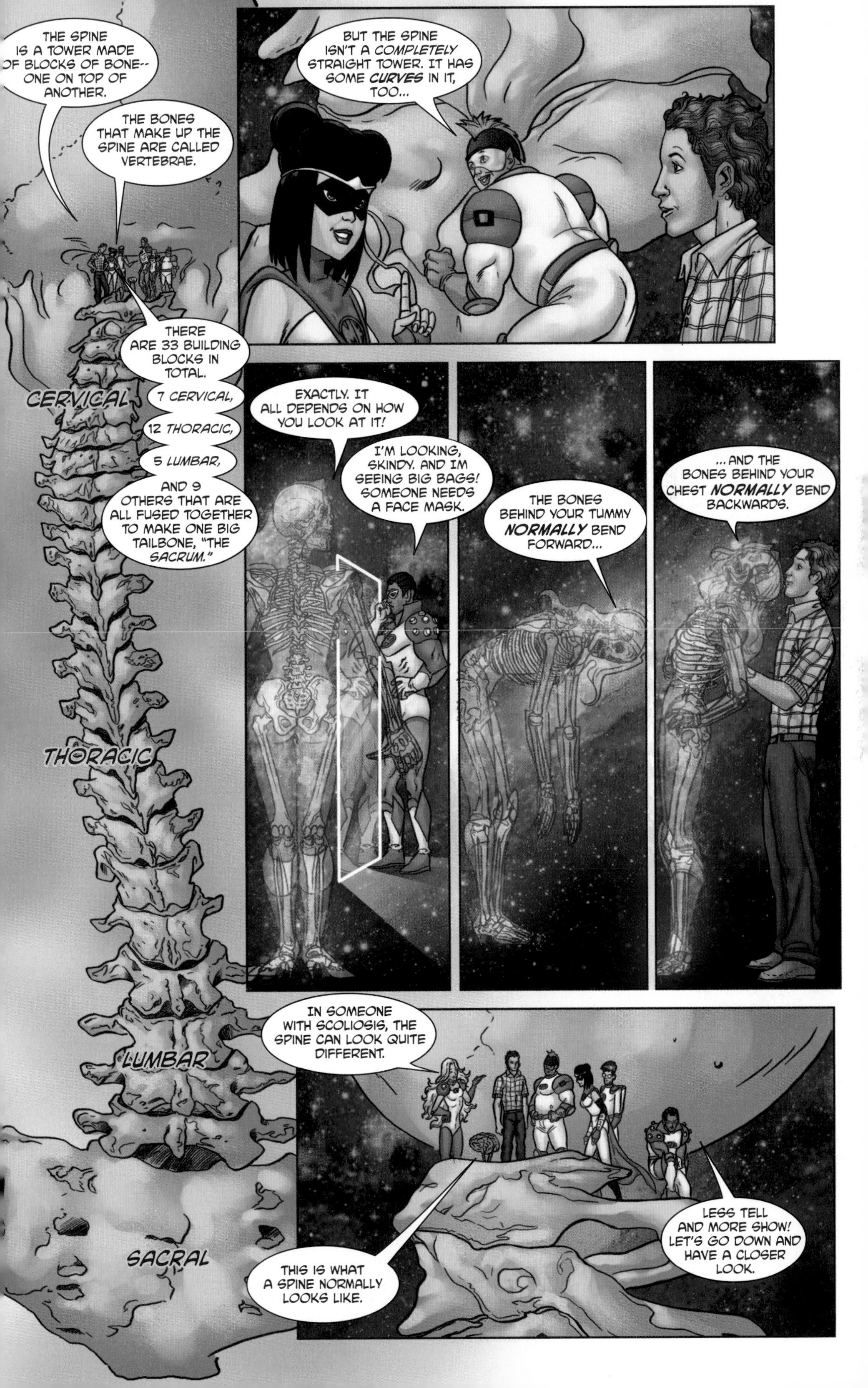
THE SPINE IS A TOWER MADE OF BLOCKS OF BONE-- ONE ON TOP OF ANOTHER.
THE BONES THAT MAKE UP THE SPINE ARE CALLED VERTEBRAE.
BUT THE SPINE ISN'T A COMPLETELY STRAIGHT TOWER. IT HAS SOME CURVES IN IT, TOO...
THERE ARE 33 BUILDING BLOCKS IN TOTAL.
7 CERVICAL,
12 THORACIC,
5 LUMBAR,
AND 9 OTHERS THAT ARE ALL FUSED TOGETHER TO MAKE ONE BIG TAILBONE, "THE SACRUM."
CERVICAL
EXACTLY. IT ALL DEPENDS ON HOW YOU LOOK AT IT!
I'M LOOKING, SKINDY. AND IM SEEING BIG BAGS! SOMEONE NEEDS A FACE MASK.
THE BONES BEHIND YOUR TUMMY NORMALLY BEND FORWARD...
...AND THE BONES BEHIND YOUR CHEST NORMALLY BEND BACKWARDS.
THORACIC
LUMBAR
IN SOMEONE WITH SCOLIOSIS, THE SPINE CAN LOOK QUITE DIFFERENT.
LESS TELL AND MORE SHOW! LET'S GO DOWN AND HAVE A CLOSER LOOK.
SACRAL
THIS IS WHAT A SPINE NORMALLY LOOKS LIKE.

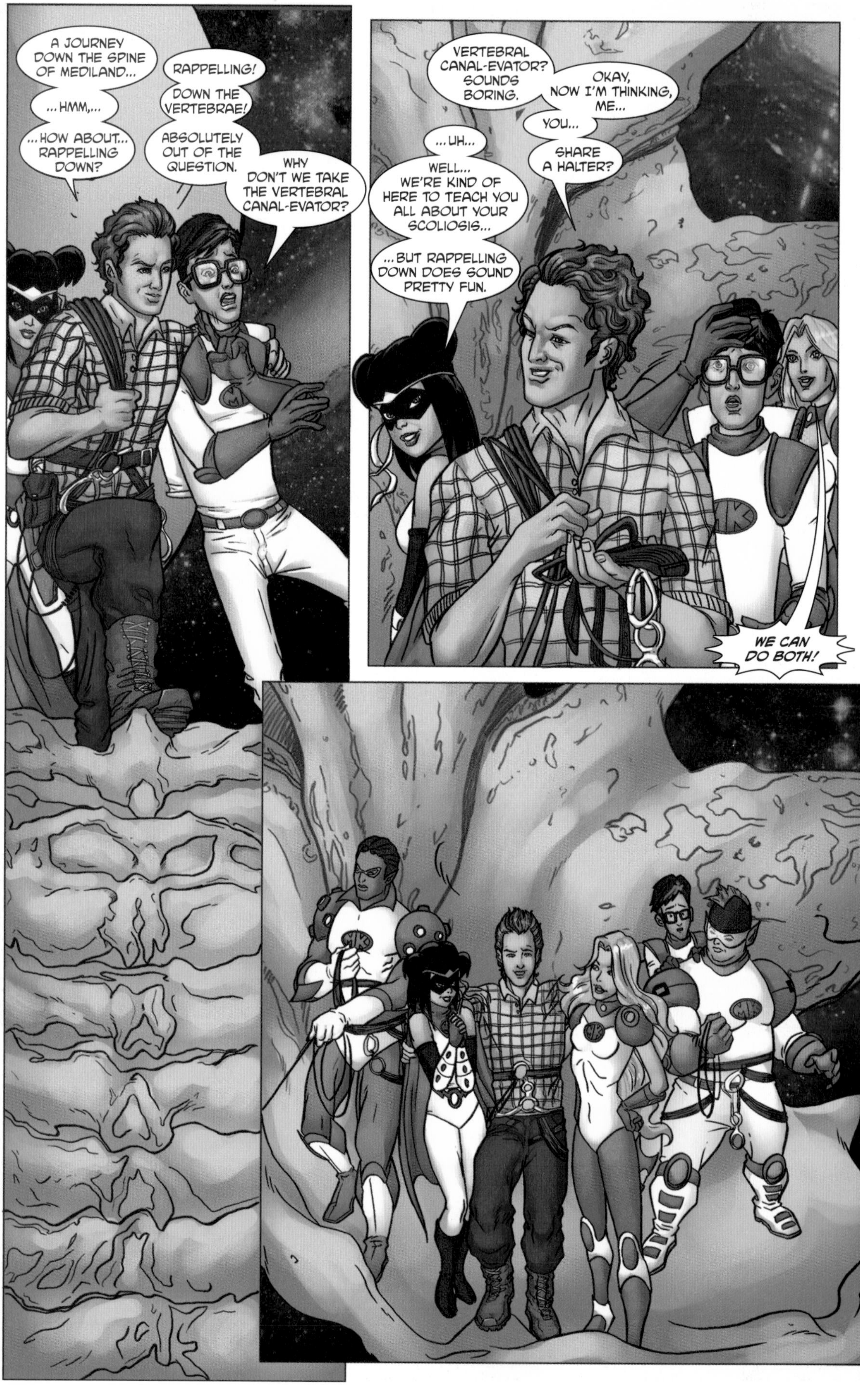
A JOURNEY DOWN THE SPINE OF MEDILAND...
...HMM,...
...HOW ABOUT... RAPPELLING DOWN?
RAPPELLING! DOWN THE VERTEBRAE!
ABSOLUTELY OUT OF THE QUESTION.
WHY DON'T WE TAKE THE VERTEBRAL CANAL-EVATOR?
VERTEBRAL CANAL-EVATOR? SOUNDS BORING.
...UH...
WELL... WE'RE KIND OF HERE TO TEACH YOU ALL ABOUT YOUR SCOLIOSIS...
...BUT RAPPELLING DOWN DOES SOUND PRETTY FUN.
OKAY, NOW I'M THINKING, ME...
YOU...
SHARE A HALTER?
WE CAN DO BOTH!

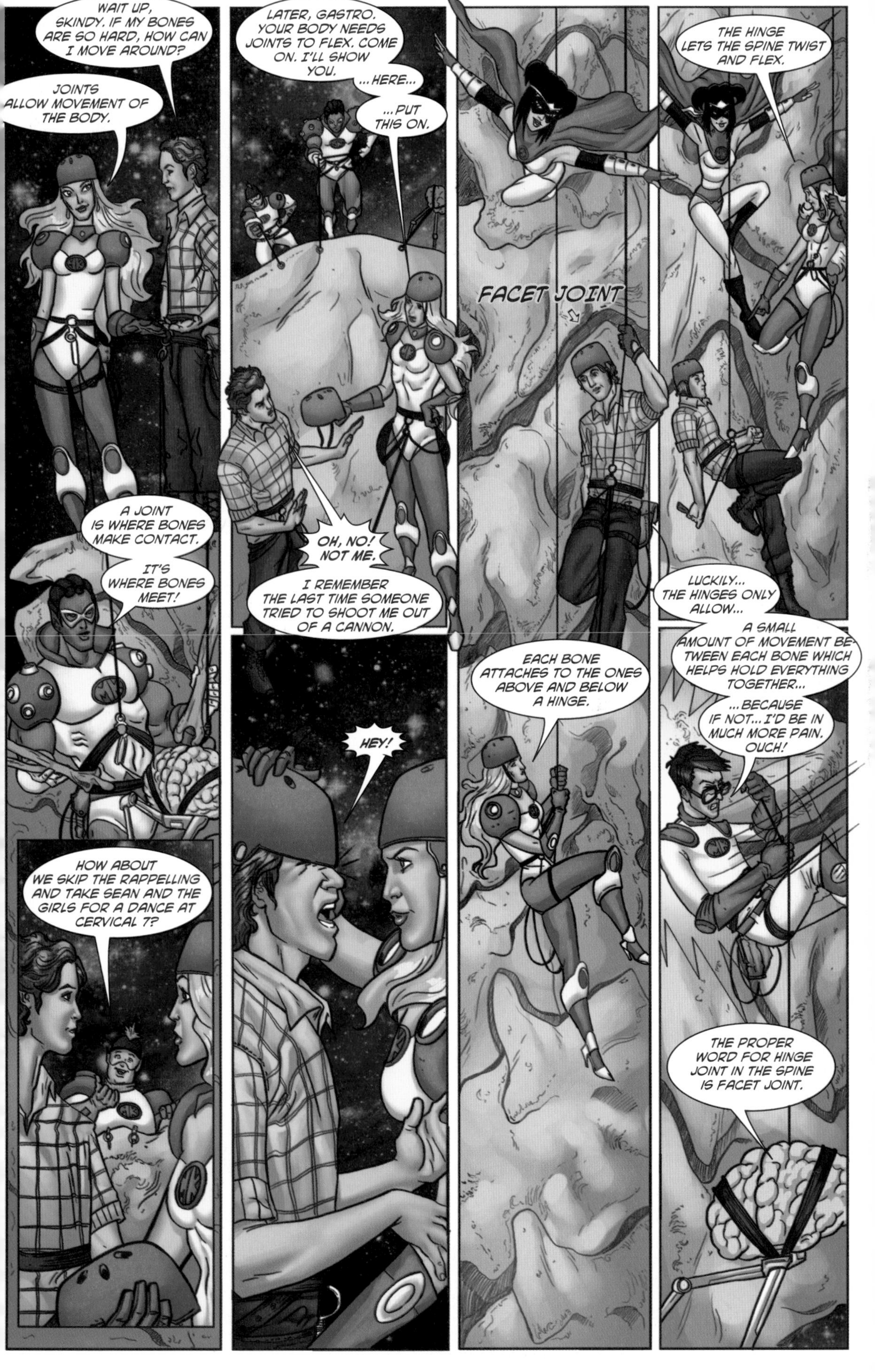
WAIT UP, SKINDY. IF MY BONES ARE SO HARD, HOW CAN I MOVE AROUND?
JOINTS ALLOW MOVEMENT OF THE BODY.
A JOINT IS WHERE BONES MAKE CONTACT.
IT'S WHERE BONES MEET!
HOW ABOUT WE SKIP THE RAPPELLING AND TAKE SEAN AND THE GIRLS FOR A DANCE AT CERVICAL 7?
LATER, GASTRO. YOUR BODY NEEDS JOINTS TO FLEX. COME ON. I'LL SHOW YOU.
...HERE...
...PUT THIS ON.
OH, NO! NOT ME.
I REMEMBER THE LAST TIME SOMEONE TRIED TO SHOOT ME OUT OF A CANNON.
HEY!
FACET JOINT
EACH BONE ATTACHES TO THE ONES ABOVE AND BELOW A HINGE.
THE HINGE LETS THE SPINE TWIST AND FLEX.
LUCKILY... THE HINGES ONLY ALLOW...
A SMALL AMOUNT OF MOVEMENT BETWEEN EACH BONE WHICH HELPS HOLD EVERYTHING TOGETHER...
...BECAUSE IF NOT... I'D BE IN MUCH MORE PAIN. OUCH!
THE PROPER WORD FOR HINGE JOINT IN THE SPINE IS FACET JOINT.

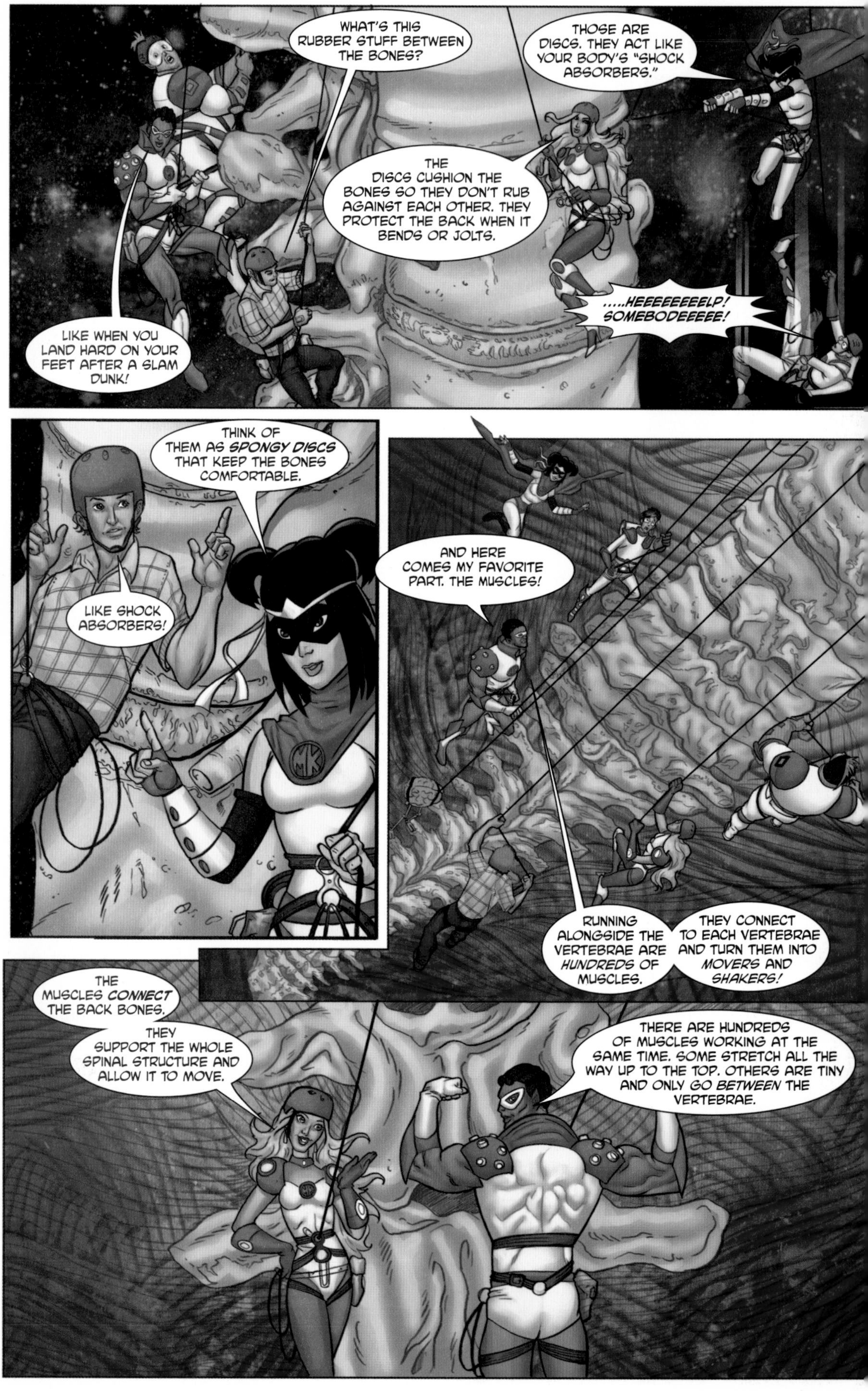
WHAT'S THIS RUBBER STUFF BETWEEN THE BONES?
THOSE ARE DISCS. THEY ACT LIKE YOUR BODY'S "SHOCK ABSORBERS."
THE DISCS CUSHION THE BONES SO THEY DON'T RUB AGAINST EACH OTHER. THEY PROTECT THE BACK WHEN IT BENDS OR JOLTS.
LIKE WHEN YOU LAND HARD ON YOUR FEET AFTER A SLAM DUNK!
.....HEEEEEEEELP! SOMEBODEEEEE!
THINK OF THEM AS *SPONGY DISCS* THAT KEEP THE BONES COMFORTABLE.
LIKE SHOCK ABSORBERS!
AND HERE COMES MY FAVORITE PART. THE MUSCLES!
RUNNING ALONGSIDE THE VERTEBRAE ARE *HUNDREDS* OF MUSCLES.
THEY CONNECT TO EACH VERTEBRAE AND TURN THEM INTO *MOVERS* AND *SHAKERS!*
THE MUSCLES *CONNECT* THE BACK BONES.
THEY SUPPORT THE WHOLE SPINAL STRUCTURE AND ALLOW IT TO MOVE.
THERE ARE HUNDREDS OF MUSCLES WORKING AT THE SAME TIME. SOME STRETCH ALL THE WAY UP TO THE TOP. OTHERS ARE TINY AND ONLY GO *BETWEEN* THE VERTEBRAE.

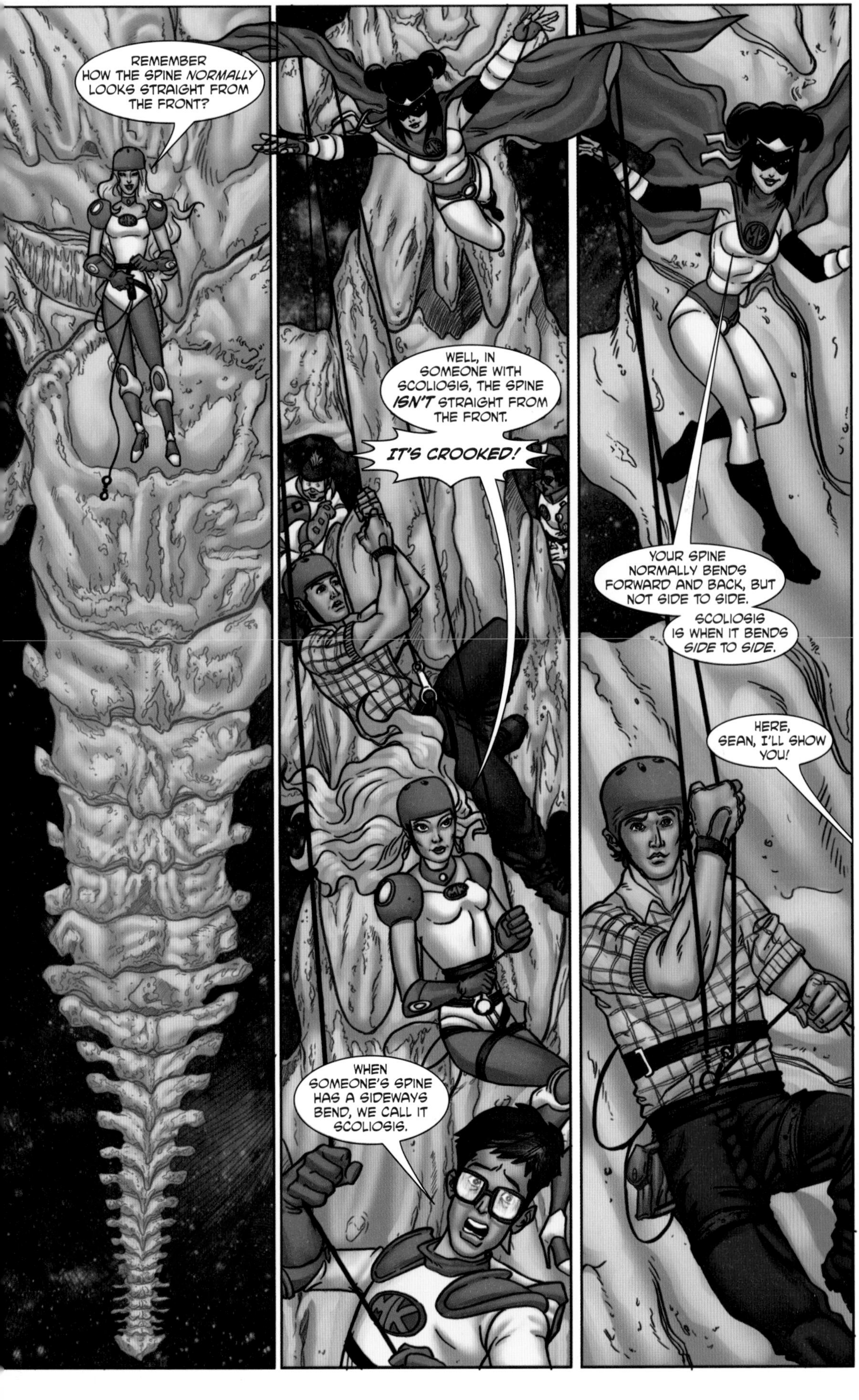
REMEMBER HOW THE SPINE *NORMALLY* LOOKS STRAIGHT FROM THE FRONT?
WELL, IN SOMEONE WITH SCOLIOSIS, THE SPINE *ISN'T* STRAIGHT FROM THE FRONT.
IT'S CROOKED!
WHEN SOMEONE'S SPINE HAS A SIDEWAYS BEND, WE CALL IT SCOLIOSIS.
YOUR SPINE NORMALLY BENDS FORWARD AND BACK, BUT NOT SIDE TO SIDE.
SCOLIOSIS IS WHEN IT BENDS *SIDE TO SIDE*.
HERE, SEAN, I'LL SHOW YOU!

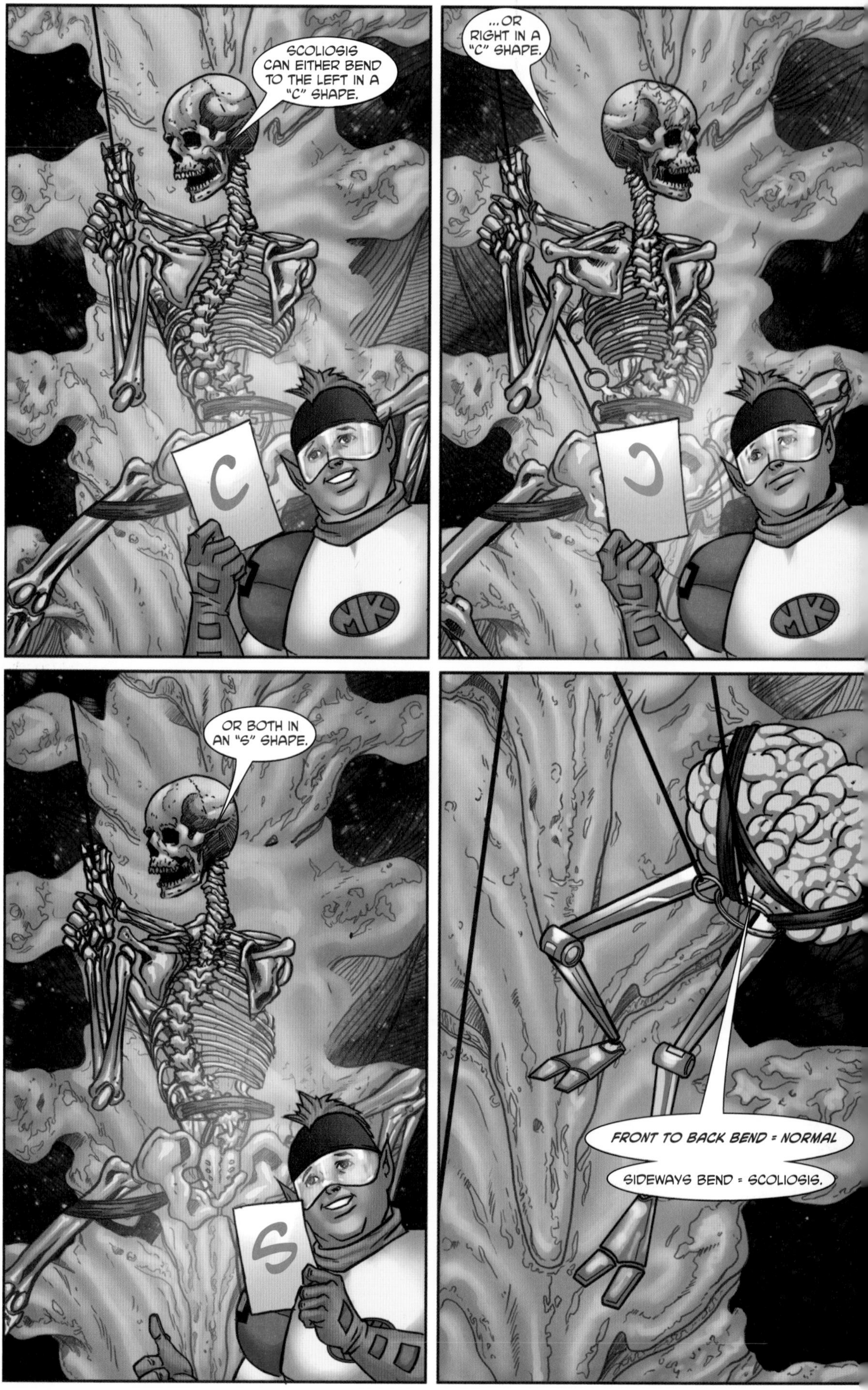
SCOLIOSIS CAN EITHER BEND TO THE LEFT IN A "C" SHAPE.
C
...OR RIGHT IN A "C" SHAPE.
OR BOTH IN AN "S" SHAPE.
S
FRONT TO BACK BEND = NORMAL
SIDEWAYS BEND = SCOLIOSIS.

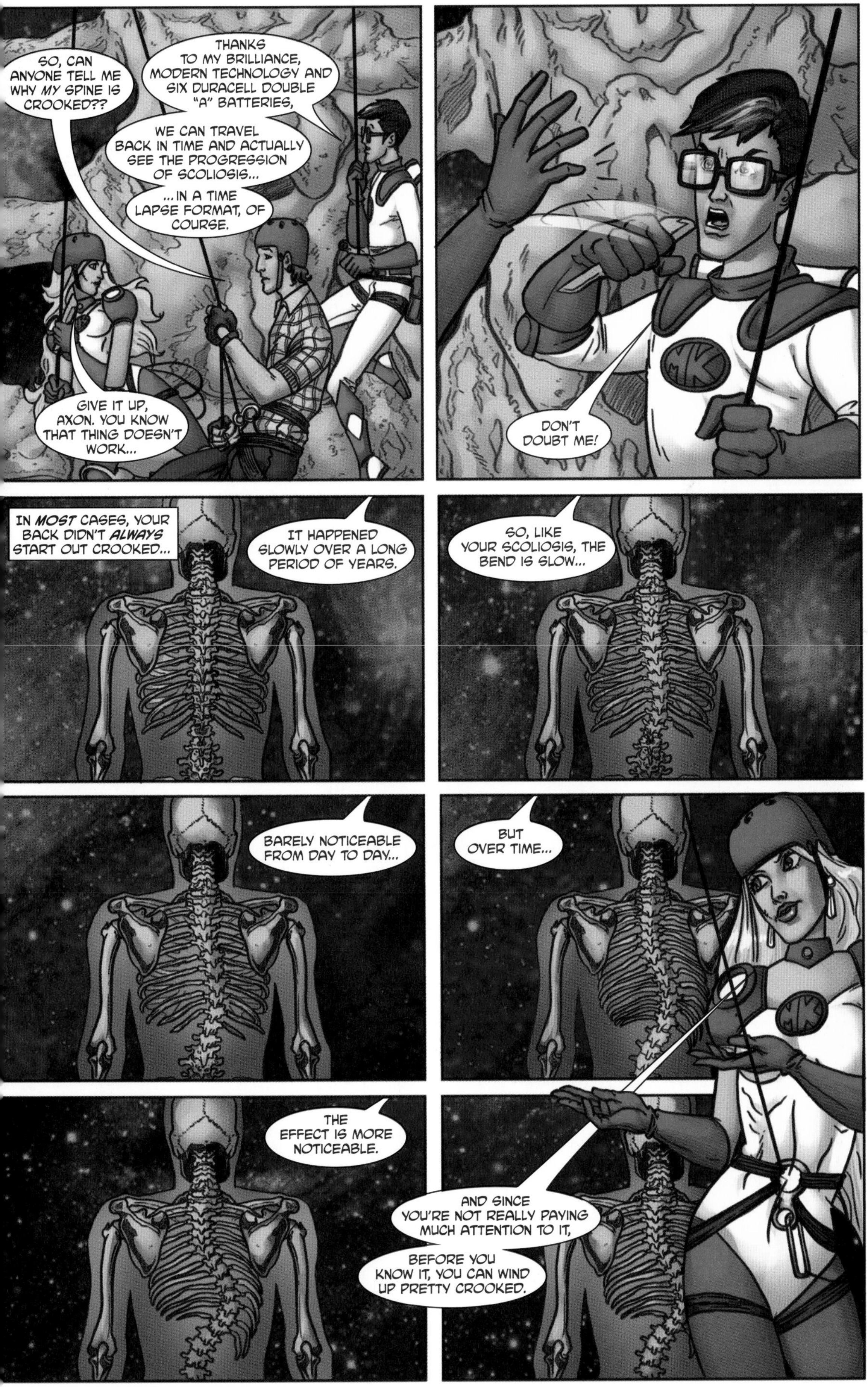
SO, CAN ANYONE TELL ME WHY *MY* SPINE IS CROOKED??
THANKS TO MY BRILLIANCE, MODERN TECHNOLOGY AND SIX DURACELL DOUBLE "A" BATTERIES,
WE CAN TRAVEL BACK IN TIME AND ACTUALLY SEE THE PROGRESSION OF SCOLIOSIS...
...IN A TIME LAPSE FORMAT, OF COURSE.
GIVE IT UP, AXON. YOU KNOW THAT THING DOESN'T WORK...
DON'T DOUBT ME!
IN *MOST* CASES, YOUR BACK DIDN'T *ALWAYS* START OUT CROOKED...
IT HAPPENED SLOWLY OVER A LONG PERIOD OF YEARS.
SO, LIKE YOUR SCOLIOSIS, THE BEND IS SLOW...
BARELY NOTICEABLE FROM DAY TO DAY...
BUT OVER TIME...
THE EFFECT IS MORE NOTICEABLE.
AND SINCE YOU'RE NOT REALLY PAYING MUCH ATTENTION TO IT,
BEFORE YOU KNOW IT, YOU CAN WIND UP PRETTY CROOKED.

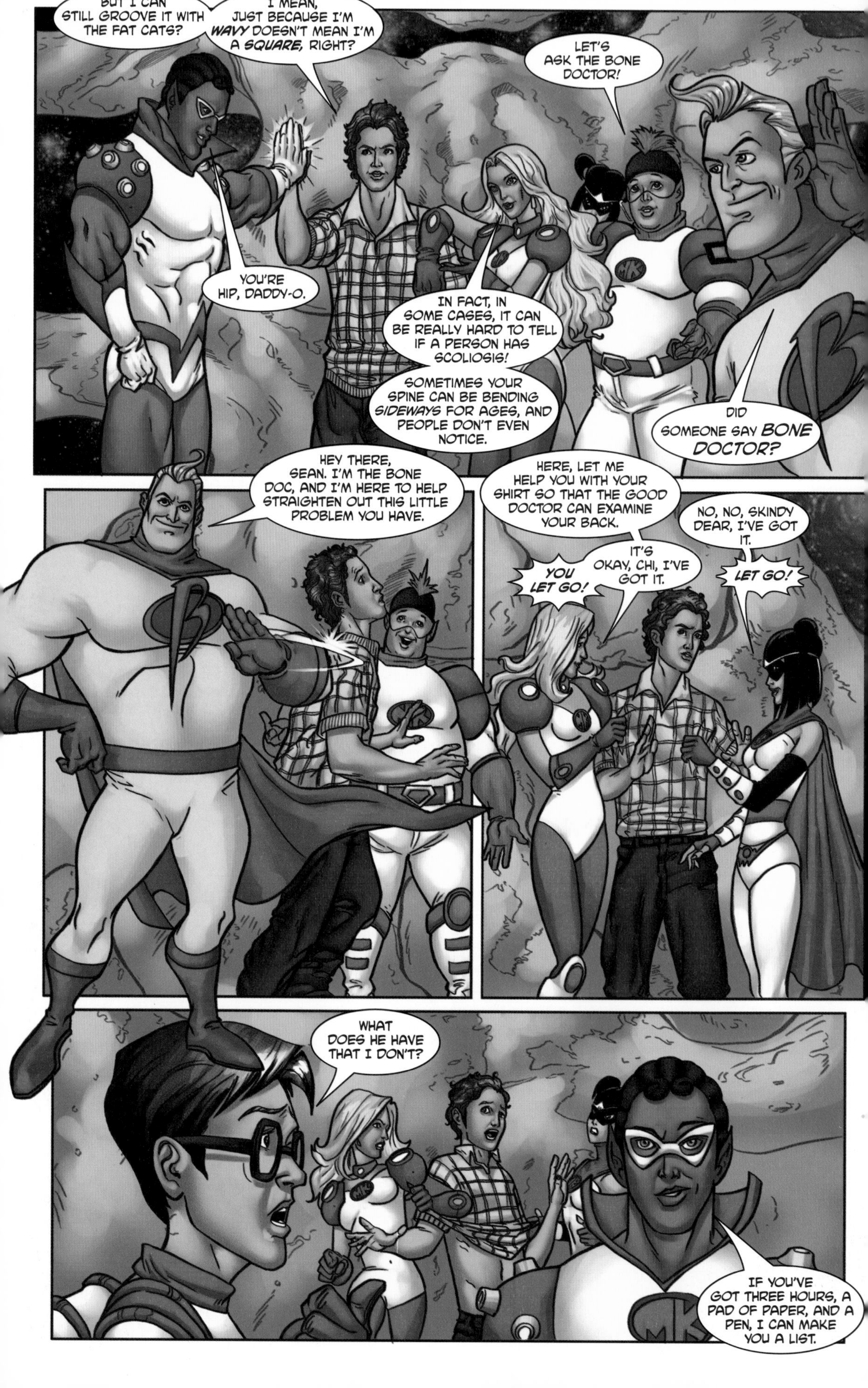
BUT I CAN STILL GROOVE IT WITH THE FAT CATS?
I MEAN, JUST BECAUSE I'M *WAVY* DOESN'T MEAN I'M A *SQUARE,* RIGHT?
YOU'RE HIP, DADDY-O.
LET'S ASK THE BONE DOCTOR!
IN FACT, IN SOME CASES, IT CAN BE REALLY HARD TO TELL IF A PERSON HAS SCOLIOSIS!
SOMETIMES YOUR SPINE CAN BE BENDING *SIDEWAYS* FOR AGES, AND PEOPLE DON'T EVEN NOTICE.
DID SOMEONE SAY *BONE DOCTOR?*
HEY THERE, SEAN. I'M THE BONE DOC, AND I'M HERE TO HELP STRAIGHTEN OUT THIS LITTLE PROBLEM YOU HAVE.
HERE, LET ME HELP YOU WITH YOUR SHIRT SO THAT THE GOOD DOCTOR CAN EXAMINE YOUR BACK.
NO, NO, SKINDY DEAR, I'VE GOT IT.
IT'S OKAY, CHI, I'VE GOT IT.
YOU LET GO!
LET GO!
WHAT DOES HE HAVE THAT I DON'T?
IF YOU'VE GOT THREE HOURS, A PAD OF PAPER, AND A PEN, I CAN MAKE YOU A LIST.

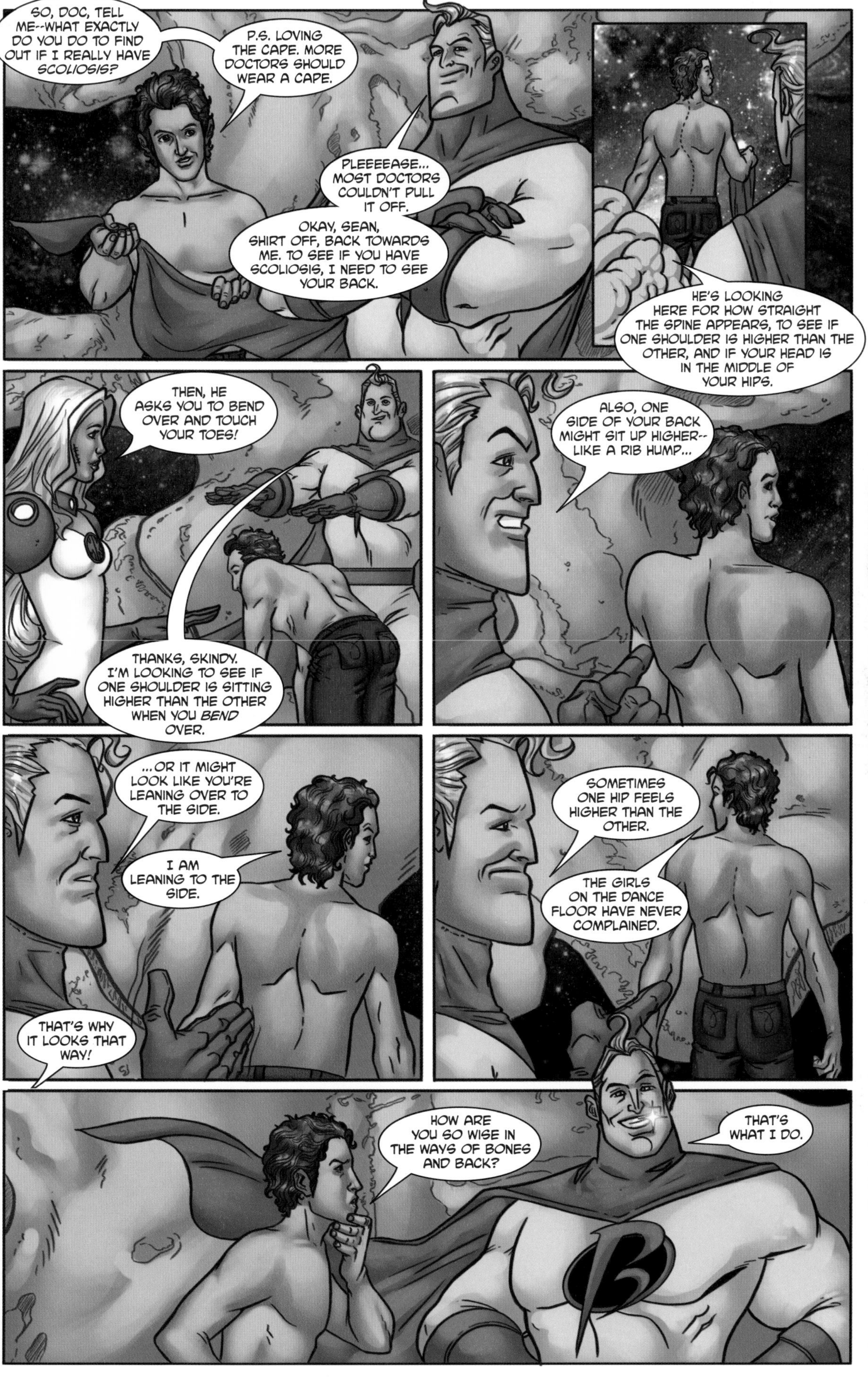
SO, DOC, TELL ME--WHAT EXACTLY DO YOU DO TO FIND OUT IF I REALLY HAVE *SCOLIOSIS*?
P.S. LOVING THE CAPE. MORE DOCTORS SHOULD WEAR A CAPE.
PLEEEEASE... MOST DOCTORS COULDN'T PULL IT OFF.
OKAY, SEAN, SHIRT OFF, BACK TOWARDS ME. TO SEE IF YOU HAVE SCOLIOSIS, I NEED TO SEE YOUR BACK.
HE'S LOOKING HERE FOR HOW STRAIGHT THE SPINE APPEARS, TO SEE IF ONE SHOULDER IS HIGHER THAN THE OTHER, AND IF YOUR HEAD IS IN THE MIDDLE OF YOUR HIPS.
THEN, HE ASKS YOU TO BEND OVER AND TOUCH YOUR TOES!
THANKS, SKINDY. I'M LOOKING TO SEE IF ONE SHOULDER IS SITTING HIGHER THAN THE OTHER WHEN YOU *BEND* OVER.
ALSO, ONE SIDE OF YOUR BACK MIGHT SIT UP HIGHER--LIKE A RIB HUMP...
...OR IT MIGHT LOOK LIKE YOU'RE LEANING OVER TO THE SIDE.
I AM LEANING TO THE SIDE.
THAT'S WHY IT LOOKS THAT WAY!
SOMETIMES ONE HIP FEELS HIGHER THAN THE OTHER.
THE GIRLS ON THE DANCE FLOOR HAVE NEVER COMPLAINED.
HOW ARE YOU SO WISE IN THE WAYS OF BONES AND BACK?
THAT'S WHAT I DO.

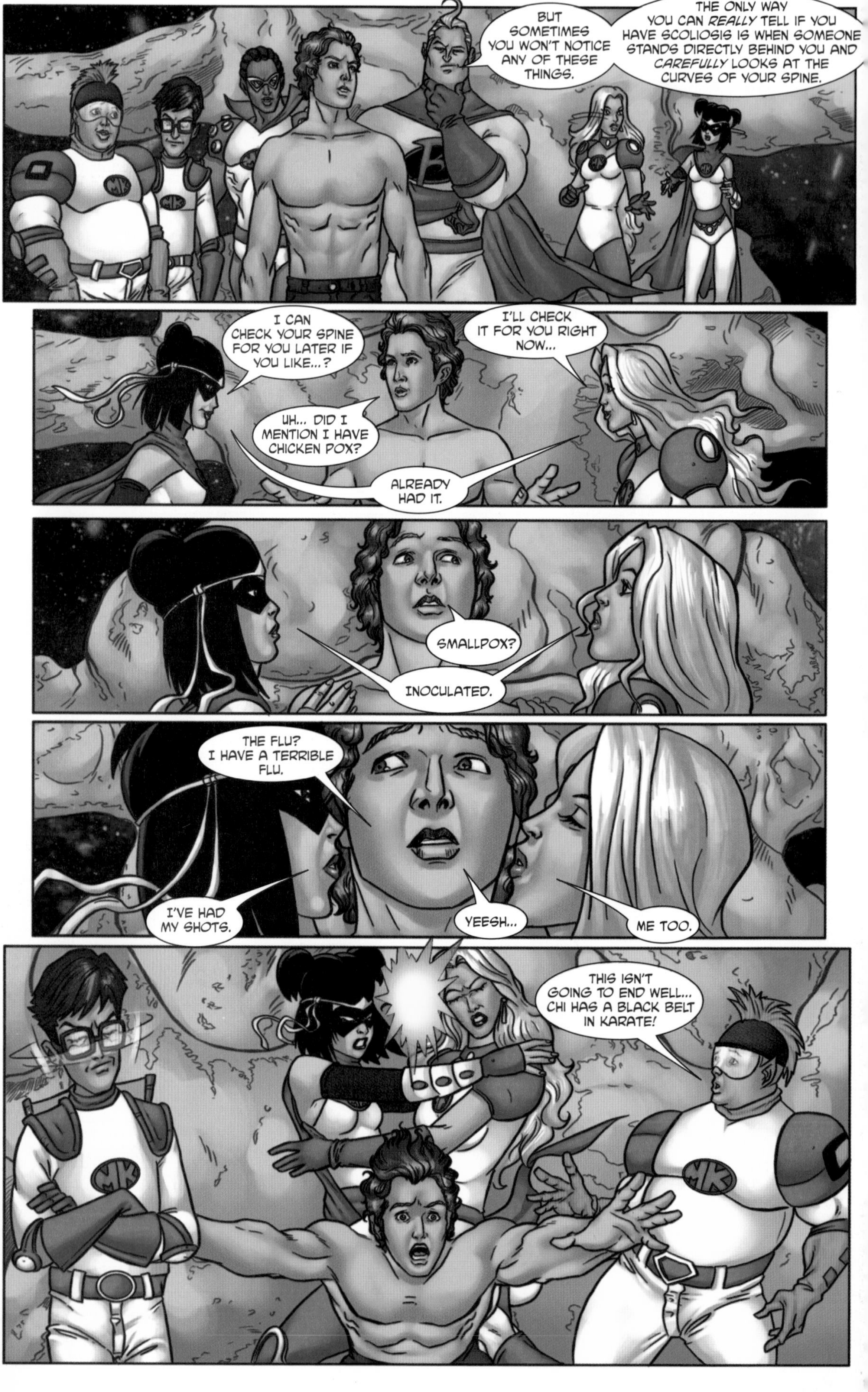
BUT SOMETIMES YOU WON'T NOTICE ANY OF THESE THINGS.
THE ONLY WAY YOU CAN *REALLY* TELL IF YOU HAVE SCOLIOSIS IS WHEN SOMEONE STANDS DIRECTLY BEHIND YOU AND *CAREFULLY* LOOKS AT THE CURVES OF YOUR SPINE.
I CAN CHECK YOUR SPINE FOR YOU LATER IF YOU LIKE...?
I'LL CHECK IT FOR YOU RIGHT NOW...
UH... DID I MENTION I HAVE CHICKEN POX?
ALREADY HAD IT.
SMALLPOX?
INOCULATED.
THE FLU? I HAVE A TERRIBLE FLU.
I'VE HAD MY SHOTS.
YEESH...
ME TOO.
THIS ISN'T GOING TO END WELL... CHI HAS A BLACK BELT IN KARATE!

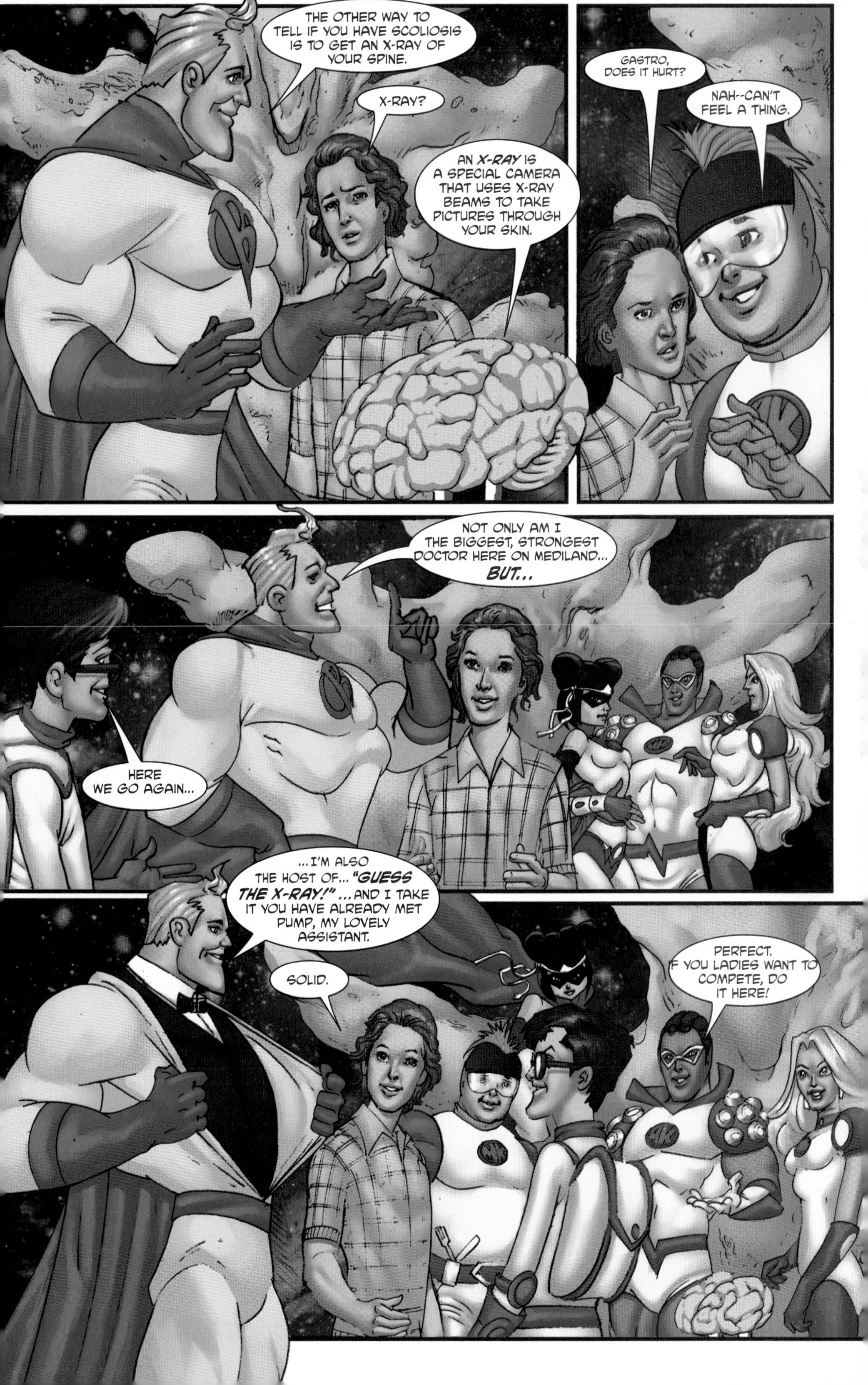
THE OTHER WAY TO TELL IF YOU HAVE SCOLIOSIS IS TO GET AN X-RAY OF YOUR SPINE.
X-RAY?
AN *X-RAY* IS A SPECIAL CAMERA THAT USES X-RAY BEAMS TO TAKE PICTURES THROUGH YOUR SKIN.
GASTRO, DOES IT HURT?
NAH--CAN'T FEEL A THING.
NOT ONLY AM I THE BIGGEST, STRONGEST DOCTOR HERE ON MEDILAND... ***BUT...***
HERE WE GO AGAIN...
...I'M ALSO THE HOST OF... ***"GUESS THE X-RAY!"*** ...AND I TAKE IT YOU HAVE ALREADY MET PUMP, MY LOVELY ASSISTANT.
SOLID.
PERFECT. IF YOU LADIES WANT TO COMPETE, DO IT HERE!

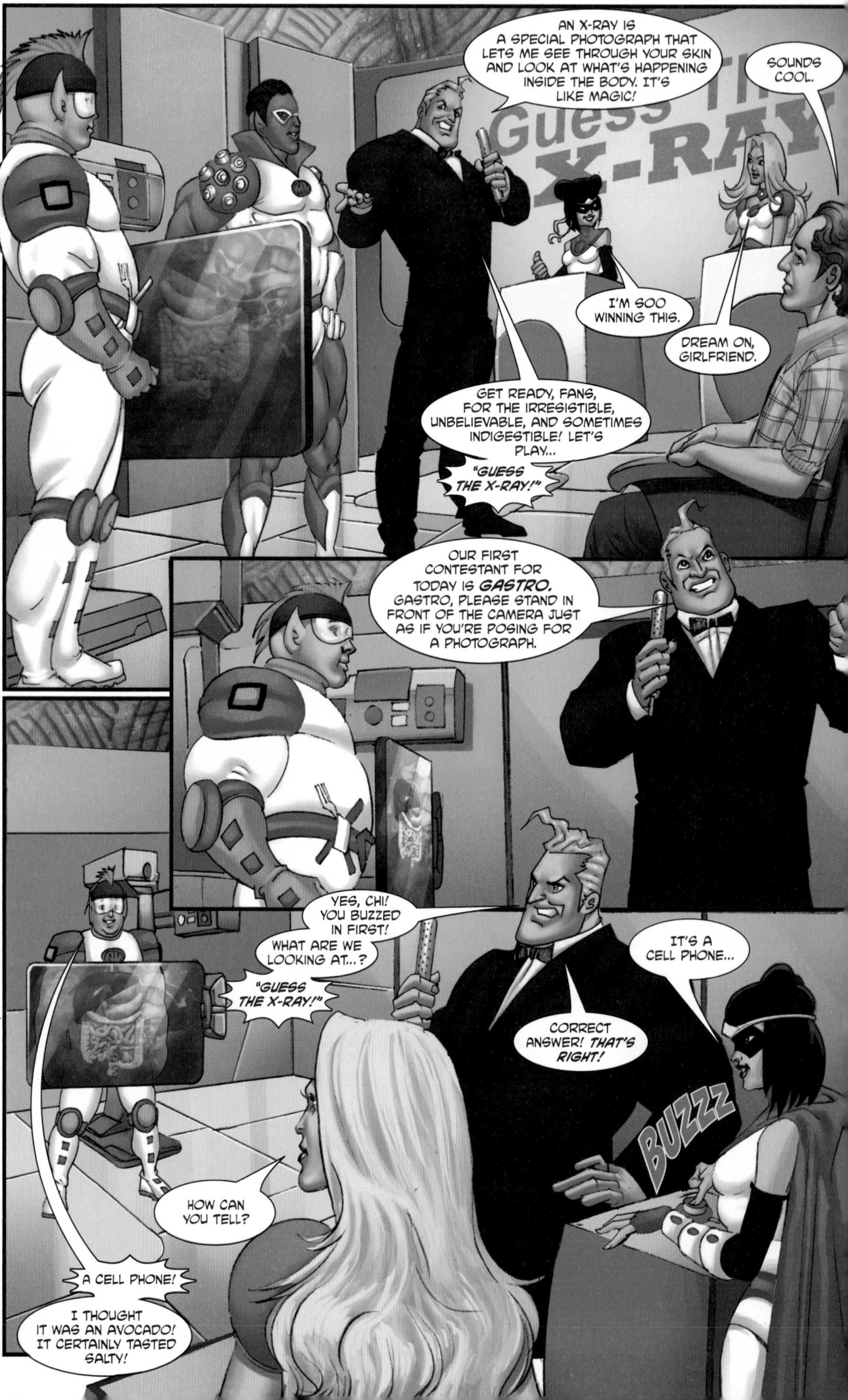
AN X-RAY IS A SPECIAL PHOTOGRAPH THAT LETS ME SEE THROUGH YOUR SKIN AND LOOK AT WHAT'S HAPPENING INSIDE THE BODY. IT'S LIKE MAGIC!
SOUNDS COOL.
Guess The X-RAY
I'M SOO WINNING THIS.
DREAM ON, GIRLFRIEND.
GET READY, FANS, FOR THE IRRESISTIBLE, UNBELIEVABLE, AND SOMETIMES INDIGESTIBLE! LET'S PLAY...
"GUESS THE X-RAY!"
OUR FIRST CONTESTANT FOR TODAY IS GASTRO. GASTRO, PLEASE STAND IN FRONT OF THE CAMERA JUST AS IF YOU'RE POSING FOR A PHOTOGRAPH.
YES, CHI! YOU BUZZED IN FIRST!
WHAT ARE WE LOOKING AT...?
"GUESS THE X-RAY!"
IT'S A CELL PHONE...
CORRECT ANSWER! THAT'S RIGHT!
BUZZZ
HOW CAN YOU TELL?
A CELL PHONE!
I THOUGHT IT WAS AN AVOCADO! IT CERTAINLY TASTED SALTY!

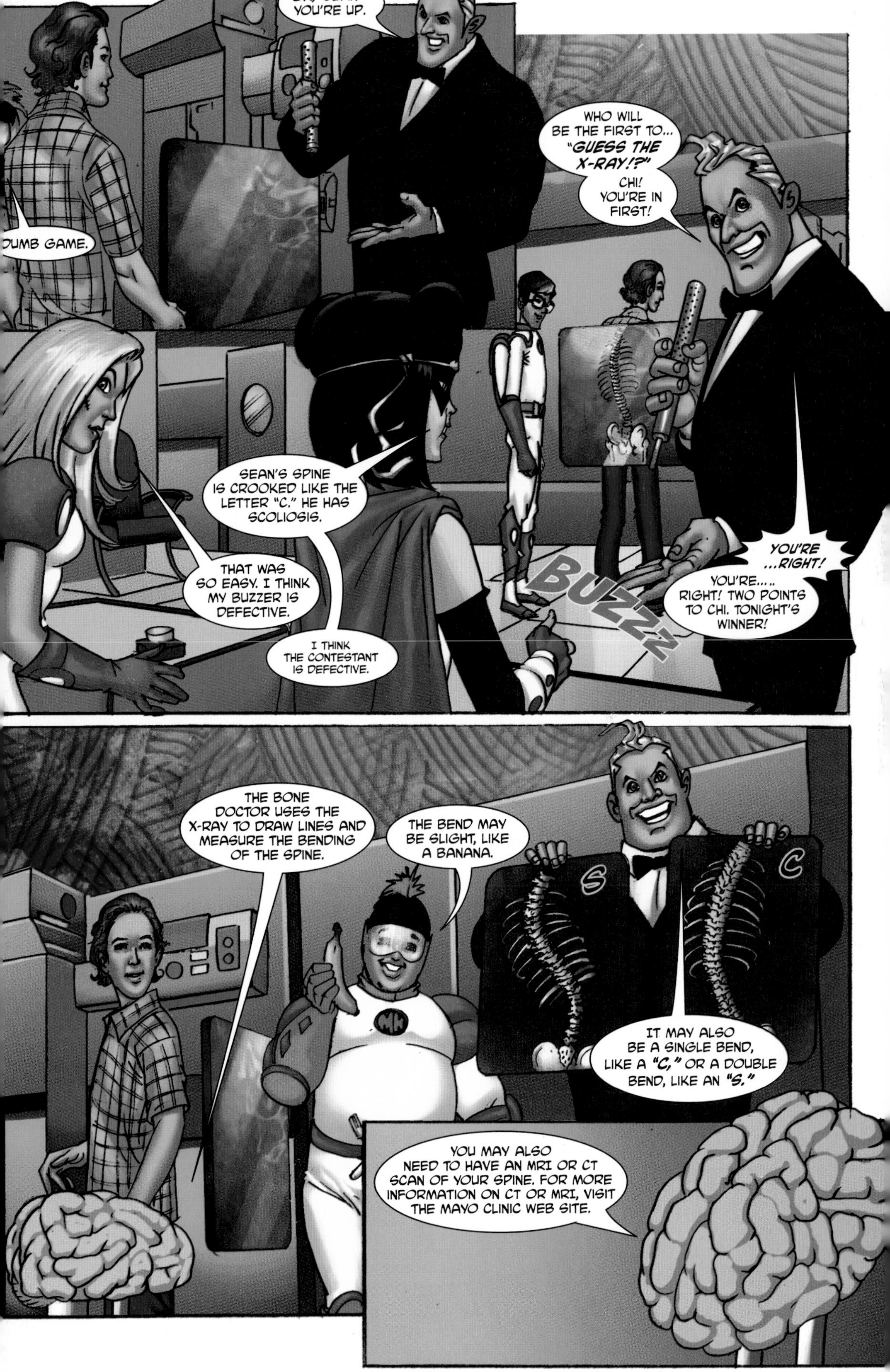

OK, SEAN-- YOU'RE UP.
DUMB GAME.
WHO WILL BE THE FIRST TO... *"GUESS THE X-RAY!?"*
CHI! YOU'RE IN FIRST!
SEAN'S SPINE IS CROOKED LIKE THE LETTER "C." HE HAS SCOLIOSIS.
THAT WAS SO EASY. I THINK MY BUZZER IS DEFECTIVE.
I THINK THE CONTESTANT IS DEFECTIVE.
BUZZZ
YOU'RE ...RIGHT!
YOU'RE..... RIGHT! TWO POINTS TO CHI. TONIGHT'S WINNER!
THE BONE DOCTOR USES THE X-RAY TO DRAW LINES AND MEASURE THE BENDING OF THE SPINE.
THE BEND MAY BE SLIGHT, LIKE A BANANA.
S
C
IT MAY ALSO BE A SINGLE BEND, LIKE A *"C,"* OR A DOUBLE BEND, LIKE AN *"S."*
YOU MAY ALSO NEED TO HAVE AN MRI OR CT SCAN OF YOUR SPINE. FOR MORE INFORMATION ON CT OR MRI, VISIT THE MAYO CLINIC WEB SITE.

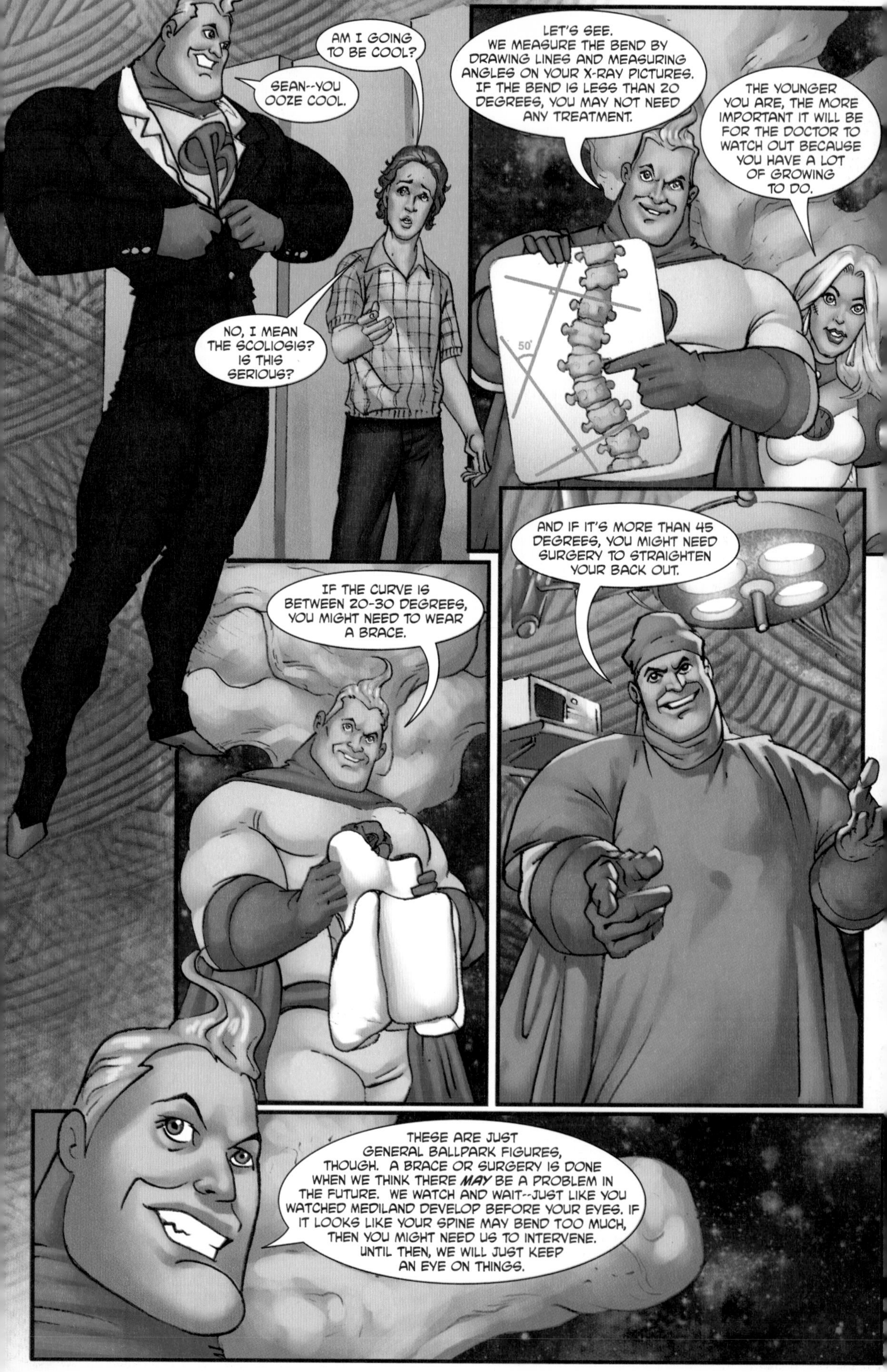

AM I GOING TO BE COOL?
SEAN--YOU OOZE COOL.
NO, I MEAN THE SCOLIOSIS? IS THIS SERIOUS?
LET'S SEE. WE MEASURE THE BEND BY DRAWING LINES AND MEASURING ANGLES ON YOUR X-RAY PICTURES. IF THE BEND IS LESS THAN 20 DEGREES, YOU MAY NOT NEED ANY TREATMENT.
THE YOUNGER YOU ARE, THE MORE IMPORTANT IT WILL BE FOR THE DOCTOR TO WATCH OUT BECAUSE YOU HAVE A LOT OF GROWING TO DO.
50°
IF THE CURVE IS BETWEEN 20-30 DEGREES, YOU MIGHT NEED TO WEAR A BRACE.
AND IF IT'S MORE THAN 45 DEGREES, YOU MIGHT NEED SURGERY TO STRAIGHTEN YOUR BACK OUT.
THESE ARE JUST GENERAL BALLPARK FIGURES, THOUGH. A BRACE OR SURGERY IS DONE WHEN WE THINK THERE *MAY* BE A PROBLEM IN THE FUTURE. WE WATCH AND WAIT--JUST LIKE YOU WATCHED MEDILAND DEVELOP BEFORE YOUR EYES. IF IT LOOKS LIKE YOUR SPINE MAY BEND TOO MUCH, THEN YOU MIGHT NEED US TO INTERVENE. UNTIL THEN, WE WILL JUST KEEP AN EYE ON THINGS.

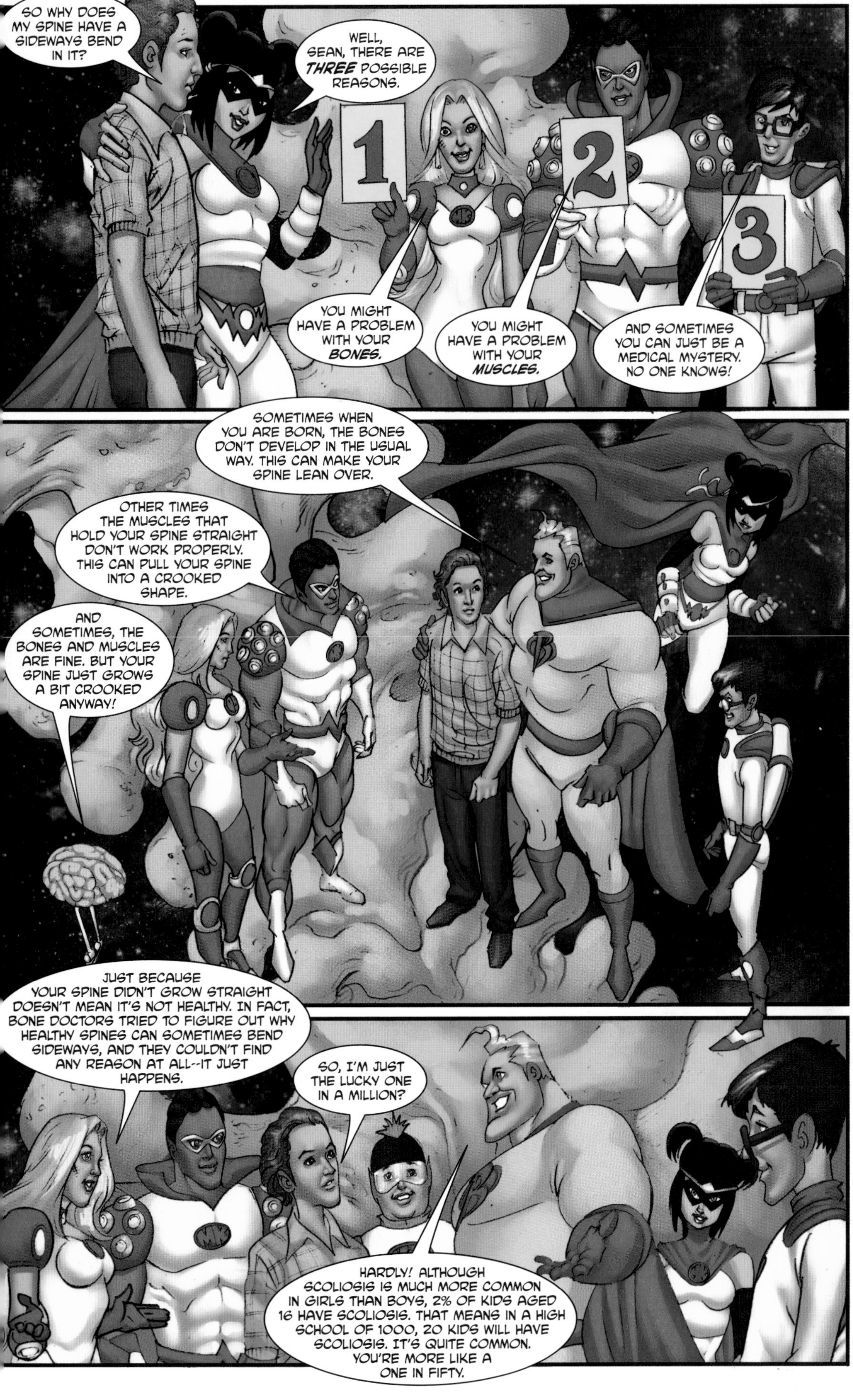
SO WHY DOES MY SPINE HAVE A SIDEWAYS BEND IN IT?
WELL, SEAN, THERE ARE *THREE* POSSIBLE REASONS.
1
2
3
YOU MIGHT HAVE A PROBLEM WITH YOUR *BONES.*
YOU MIGHT HAVE A PROBLEM WITH YOUR *MUSCLES.*
AND SOMETIMES YOU CAN JUST BE A MEDICAL MYSTERY. NO ONE KNOWS!
SOMETIMES WHEN YOU ARE BORN, THE BONES DON'T DEVELOP IN THE USUAL WAY. THIS CAN MAKE YOUR SPINE LEAN OVER.
OTHER TIMES THE MUSCLES THAT HOLD YOUR SPINE STRAIGHT DON'T WORK PROPERLY. THIS CAN PULL YOUR SPINE INTO A CROOKED SHAPE.
AND SOMETIMES, THE BONES AND MUSCLES ARE FINE. BUT YOUR SPINE JUST GROWS A BIT CROOKED ANYWAY!
JUST BECAUSE YOUR SPINE DIDN'T GROW STRAIGHT DOESN'T MEAN IT'S NOT HEALTHY. IN FACT, BONE DOCTORS TRIED TO FIGURE OUT WHY HEALTHY SPINES CAN SOMETIMES BEND SIDEWAYS, AND THEY COULDN'T FIND ANY REASON AT ALL--IT JUST HAPPENS.
SO, I'M JUST THE LUCKY ONE IN A MILLION?
HARDLY! ALTHOUGH SCOLIOSIS IS MUCH MORE COMMON IN GIRLS THAN BOYS, 2% OF KIDS AGED 16 HAVE SCOLIOSIS. THAT MEANS IN A HIGH SCHOOL OF 1000, 20 KIDS WILL HAVE SCOLIOSIS. IT'S QUITE COMMON. YOU'RE MORE LIKE A ONE IN FIFTY.

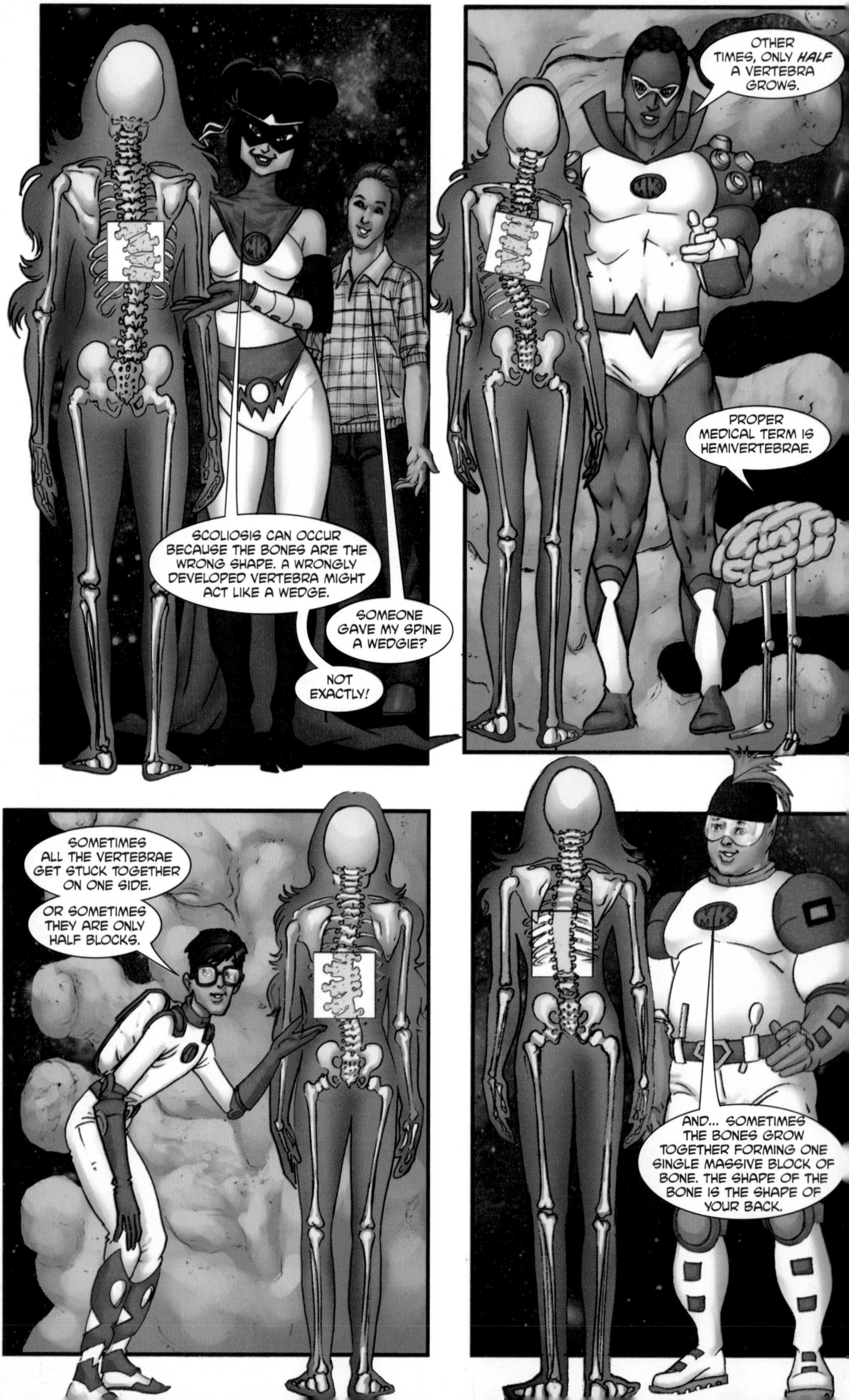
SCOLIOSIS CAN OCCUR BECAUSE THE BONES ARE THE WRONG SHAPE. A WRONGLY DEVELOPED VERTEBRA MIGHT ACT LIKE A WEDGE.
SOMEONE GAVE MY SPINE A WEDGIE?
NOT EXACTLY!
OTHER TIMES, ONLY HALF A VERTEBRA GROWS.
PROPER MEDICAL TERM IS HEMIVERTEBRAE.
SOMETIMES ALL THE VERTEBRAE GET STUCK TOGETHER ON ONE SIDE.
OR SOMETIMES THEY ARE ONLY HALF BLOCKS.
AND... SOMETIMES THE BONES GROW TOGETHER FORMING ONE SINGLE MASSIVE BLOCK OF BONE. THE SHAPE OF THE BONE IS THE SHAPE OF YOUR BACK.

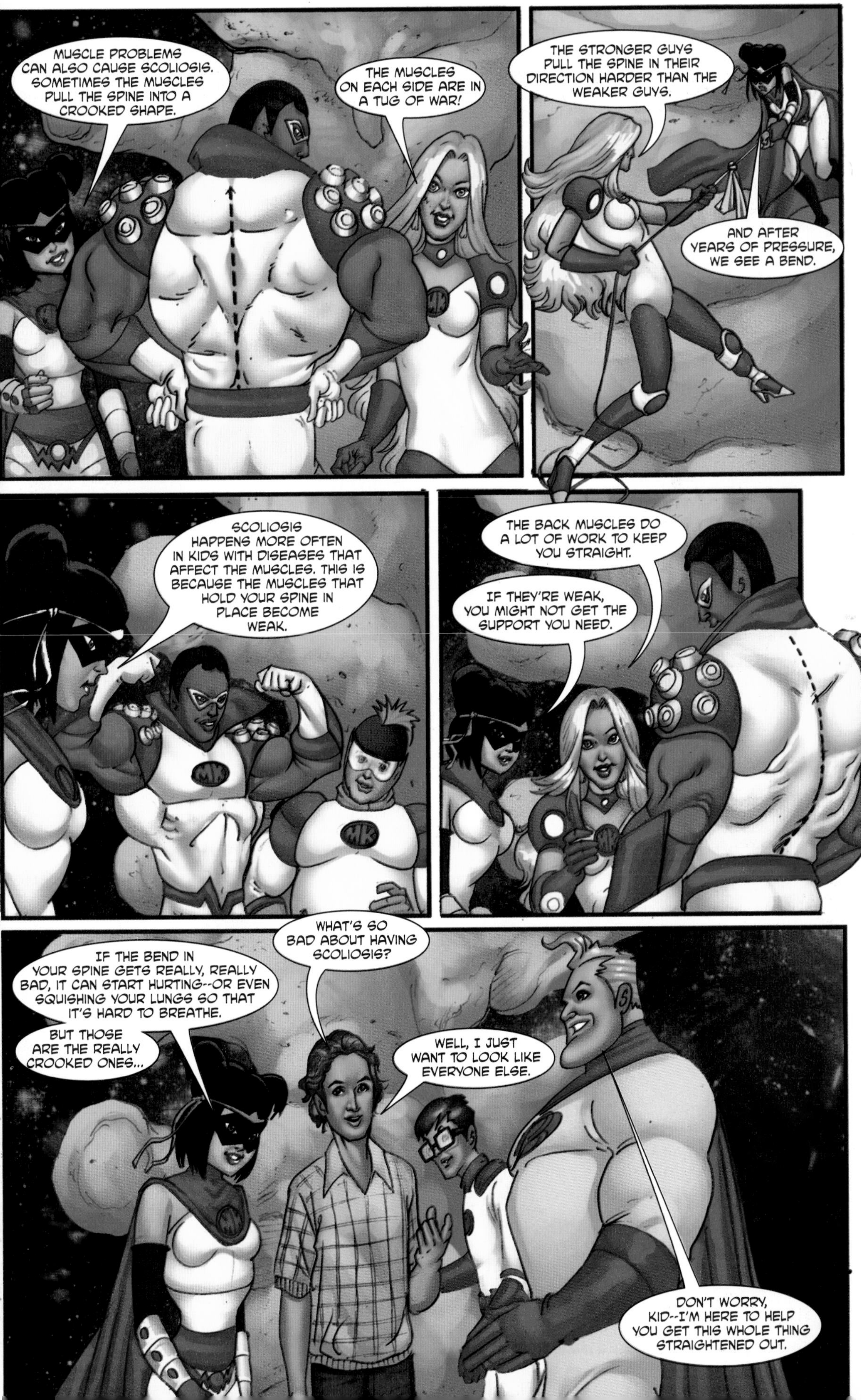
MUSCLE PROBLEMS CAN ALSO CAUSE SCOLIOSIS. SOMETIMES THE MUSCLES PULL THE SPINE INTO A CROOKED SHAPE.
THE MUSCLES ON EACH SIDE ARE IN A TUG OF WAR!
THE STRONGER GUYS PULL THE SPINE IN THEIR DIRECTION HARDER THAN THE WEAKER GUYS.
AND AFTER YEARS OF PRESSURE, WE SEE A BEND.
SCOLIOSIS HAPPENS MORE OFTEN IN KIDS WITH DISEASES THAT AFFECT THE MUSCLES. THIS IS BECAUSE THE MUSCLES THAT HOLD YOUR SPINE IN PLACE BECOME WEAK.
THE BACK MUSCLES DO A LOT OF WORK TO KEEP YOU STRAIGHT.
IF THEY'RE WEAK, YOU MIGHT NOT GET THE SUPPORT YOU NEED.
WHAT'S SO BAD ABOUT HAVING SCOLIOSIS?
IF THE BEND IN YOUR SPINE GETS REALLY, REALLY BAD, IT CAN START HURTING--OR EVEN SQUISHING YOUR LUNGS SO THAT IT'S HARD TO BREATHE.
BUT THOSE ARE THE REALLY CROOKED ONES...
WELL, I JUST WANT TO LOOK LIKE EVERYONE ELSE.
DON'T WORRY, KID--I'M HERE TO HELP YOU GET THIS WHOLE THING STRAIGHTENED OUT.

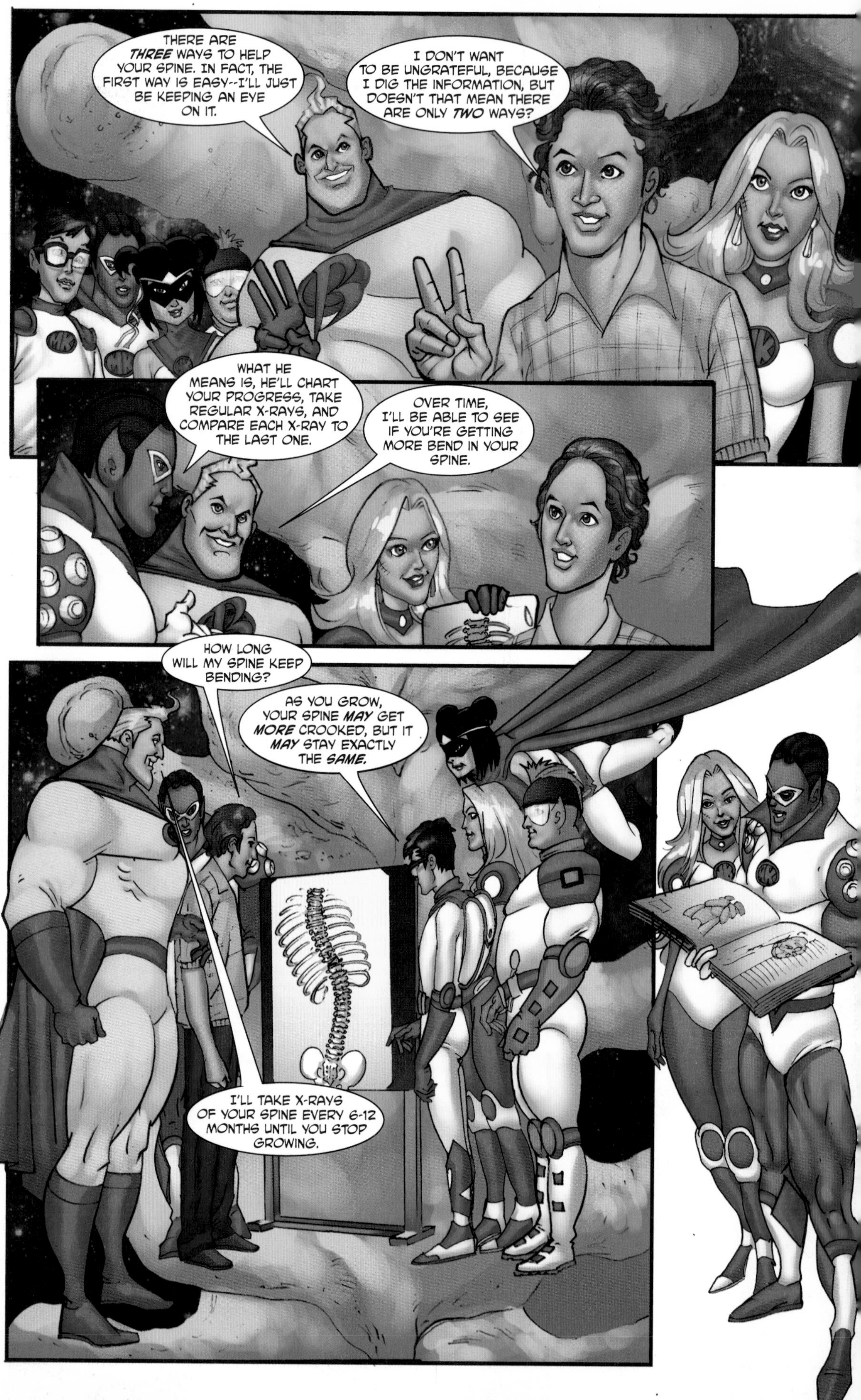
THERE ARE THREE WAYS TO HELP YOUR SPINE. IN FACT, THE FIRST WAY IS EASY--I'LL JUST BE KEEPING AN EYE ON IT.
I DON'T WANT TO BE UNGRATEFUL, BECAUSE I DIG THE INFORMATION, BUT DOESN'T THAT MEAN THERE ARE ONLY TWO WAYS?
WHAT HE MEANS IS, HE'LL CHART YOUR PROGRESS, TAKE REGULAR X-RAYS, AND COMPARE EACH X-RAY TO THE LAST ONE.
OVER TIME, I'LL BE ABLE TO SEE IF YOU'RE GETTING MORE BEND IN YOUR SPINE.
HOW LONG WILL MY SPINE KEEP BENDING?
AS YOU GROW, YOUR SPINE MAY GET MORE CROOKED, BUT IT MAY STAY EXACTLY THE SAME.
I'LL TAKE X-RAYS OF YOUR SPINE EVERY 6-12 MONTHS UNTIL YOU STOP GROWING.

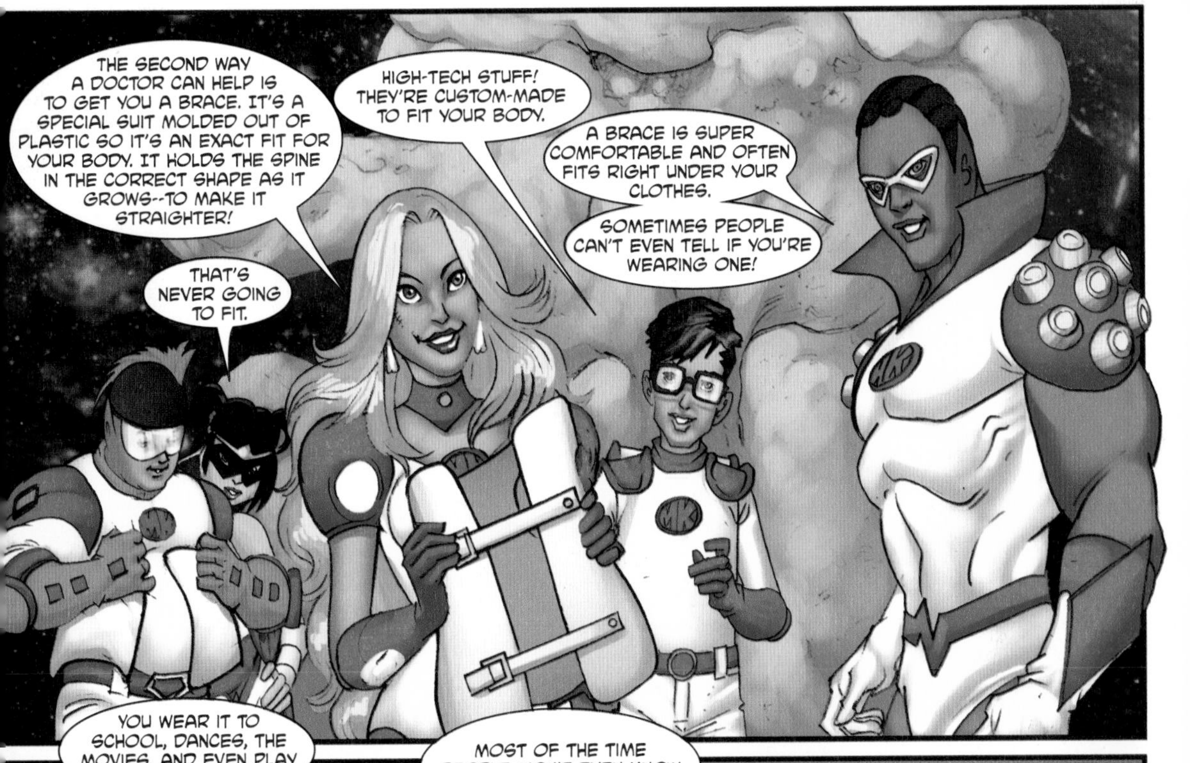
THE SECOND WAY A DOCTOR CAN HELP IS TO GET YOU A BRACE. IT'S A SPECIAL SUIT MOLDED OUT OF PLASTIC SO IT'S AN EXACT FIT FOR YOUR BODY. IT HOLDS THE SPINE IN THE CORRECT SHAPE AS IT GROWS--TO MAKE IT STRAIGHTER!
THAT'S NEVER GOING TO FIT.
HIGH-TECH STUFF! THEY'RE CUSTOM-MADE TO FIT YOUR BODY.
A BRACE IS SUPER COMFORTABLE AND OFTEN FITS RIGHT UNDER YOUR CLOTHES.
SOMETIMES PEOPLE CAN'T EVEN TELL IF YOU'RE WEARING ONE!

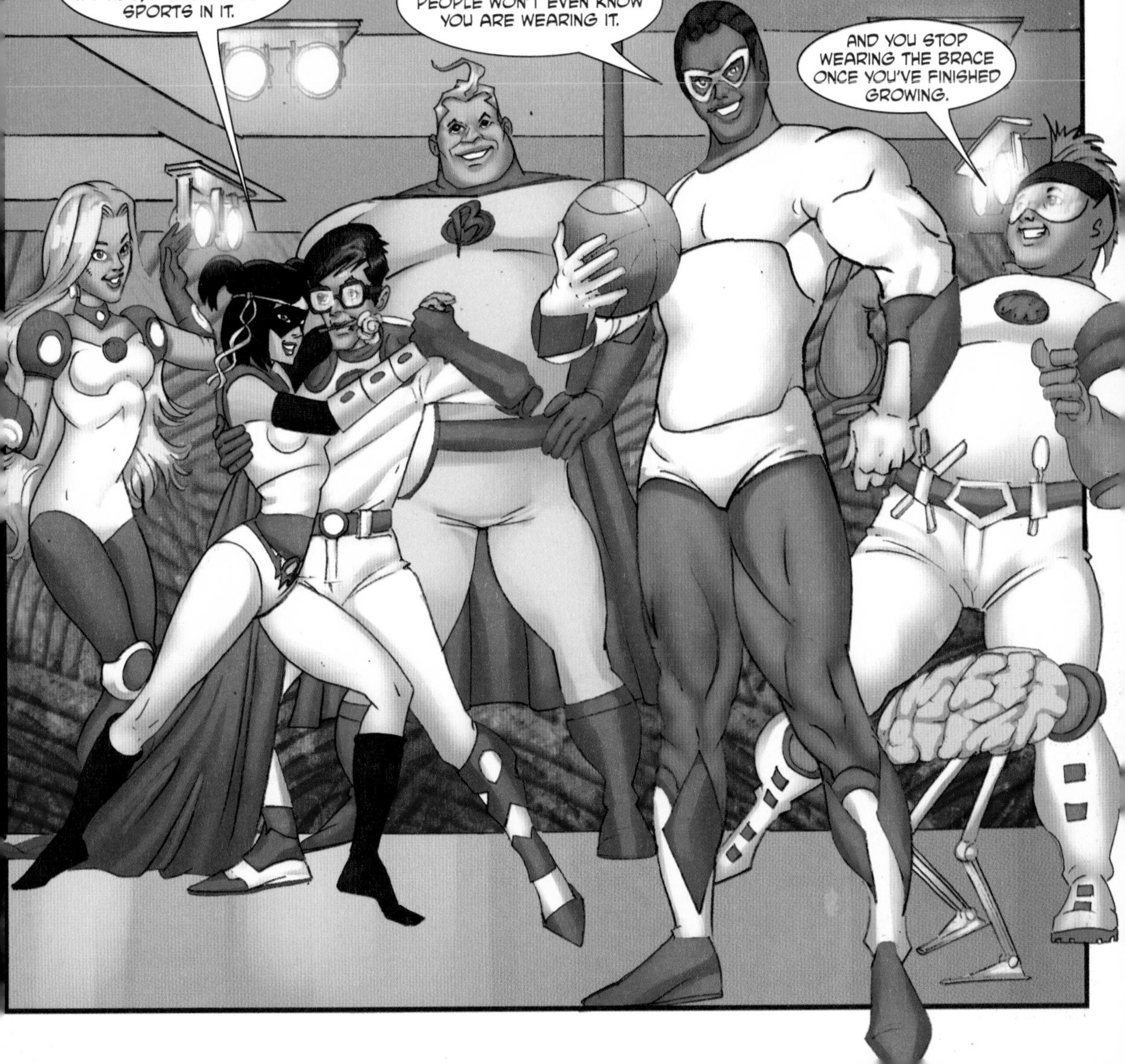
YOU WEAR IT TO SCHOOL, DANCES, THE MOVIES, AND EVEN PLAY SPORTS IN IT.
MOST OF THE TIME PEOPLE WON'T EVEN KNOW YOU ARE WEARING IT.
AND YOU STOP WEARING THE BRACE ONCE YOU'VE FINISHED GROWING.

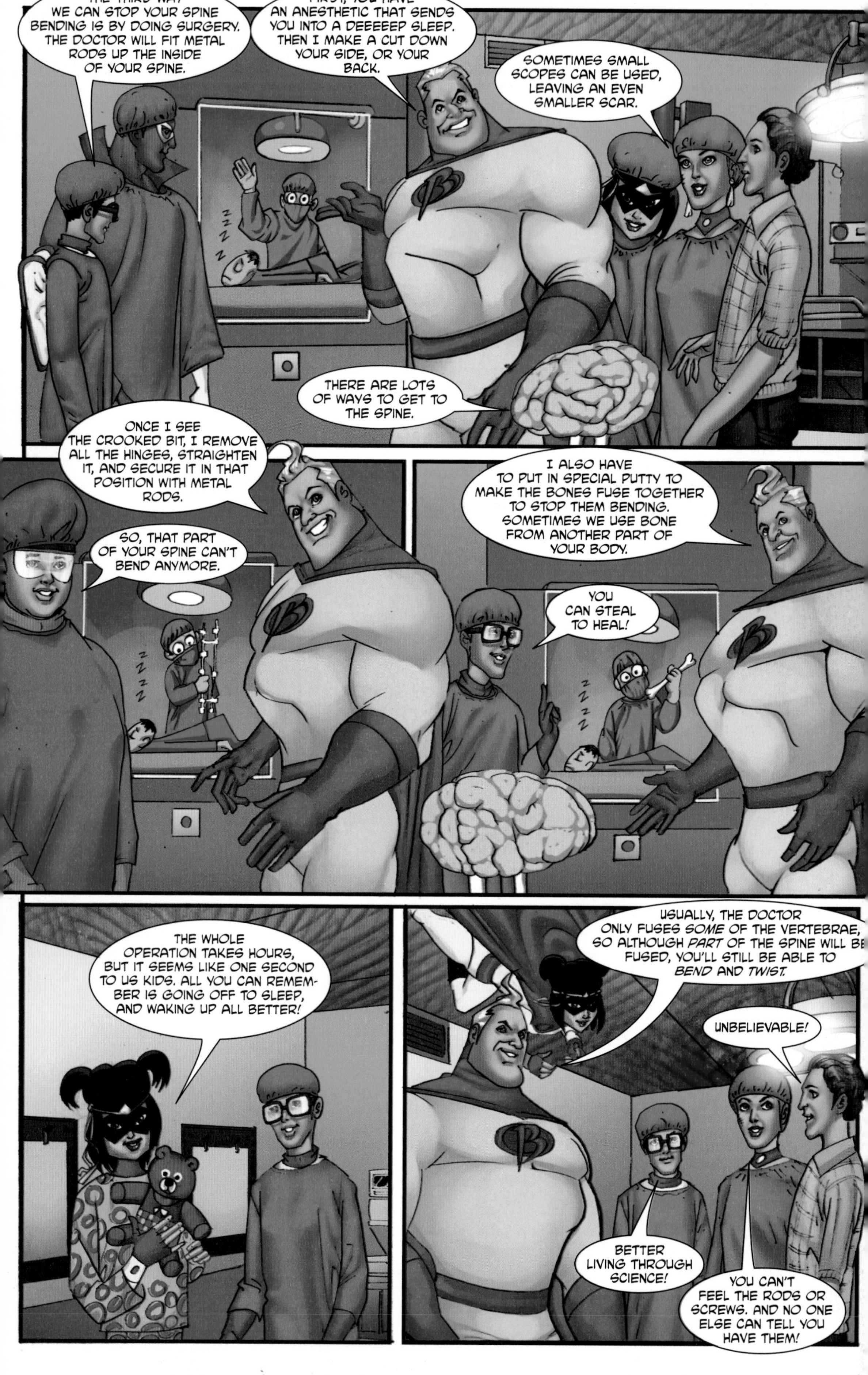
THE THIRD WAY WE CAN STOP YOUR SPINE BENDING IS BY DOING SURGERY. THE DOCTOR WILL FIT METAL RODS UP THE INSIDE OF YOUR SPINE.
FIRST, YOU HAVE AN ANESTHETIC THAT SENDS YOU INTO A DEEEEEP SLEEP. THEN I MAKE A CUT DOWN YOUR SIDE, OR YOUR BACK.
SOMETIMES SMALL SCOPES CAN BE USED, LEAVING AN EVEN SMALLER SCAR.
THERE ARE LOTS OF WAYS TO GET TO THE SPINE.
ONCE I SEE THE CROOKED BIT, I REMOVE ALL THE HINGES, STRAIGHTEN IT, AND SECURE IT IN THAT POSITION WITH METAL RODS.
SO, THAT PART OF YOUR SPINE CAN'T BEND ANYMORE.
I ALSO HAVE TO PUT IN SPECIAL PUTTY TO MAKE THE BONES FUSE TOGETHER TO STOP THEM BENDING. SOMETIMES WE USE BONE FROM ANOTHER PART OF YOUR BODY.
YOU CAN STEAL TO HEAL!
THE WHOLE OPERATION TAKES HOURS, BUT IT SEEMS LIKE ONE SECOND TO US KIDS. ALL YOU CAN REMEMBER IS GOING OFF TO SLEEP, AND WAKING UP ALL BETTER!
USUALLY, THE DOCTOR ONLY FUSES *SOME* OF THE VERTEBRAE, SO ALTHOUGH *PART* OF THE SPINE WILL BE FUSED, YOU'LL STILL BE ABLE TO *BEND* AND *TWIST*.
UNBELIEVABLE!
BETTER LIVING THROUGH SCIENCE!
YOU CAN'T FEEL THE RODS OR SCREWS. AND NO ONE ELSE CAN TELL YOU HAVE THEM!

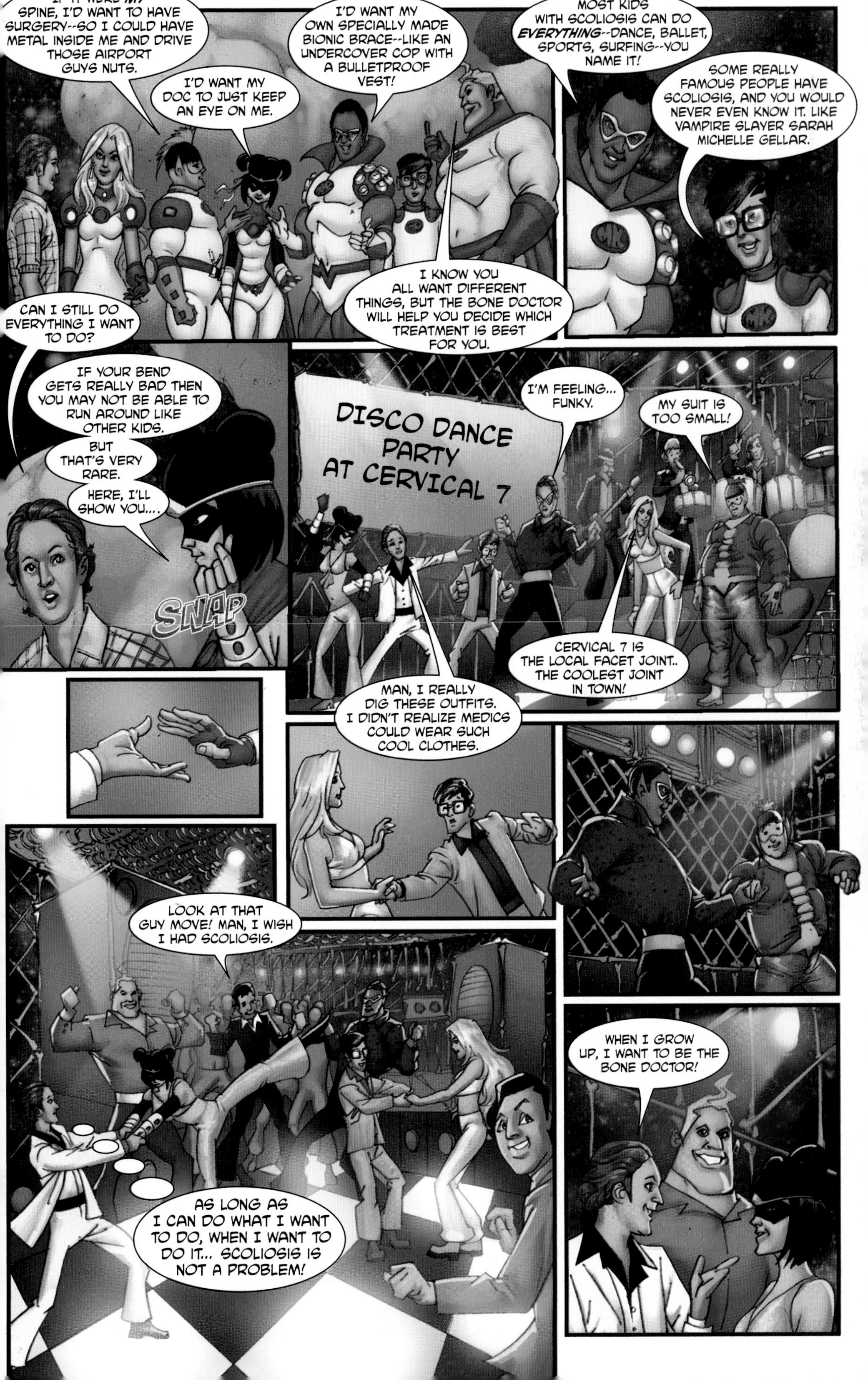
IF IT WERE MY SPINE, I'D WANT TO HAVE SURGERY--SO I COULD HAVE METAL INSIDE ME AND DRIVE THOSE AIRPORT GUYS NUTS.
I'D WANT MY DOC TO JUST KEEP AN EYE ON ME.
I'D WANT MY OWN SPECIALLY MADE BIONIC BRACE--LIKE AN UNDERCOVER COP WITH A BULLETPROOF VEST!
I KNOW YOU ALL WANT DIFFERENT THINGS, BUT THE BONE DOCTOR WILL HELP YOU DECIDE WHICH TREATMENT IS BEST FOR YOU.
MOST KIDS WITH SCOLIOSIS CAN DO EVERYTHING--DANCE, BALLET, SPORTS, SURFING--YOU NAME IT!
SOME REALLY FAMOUS PEOPLE HAVE SCOLIOSIS, AND YOU WOULD NEVER EVEN KNOW IT. LIKE VAMPIRE SLAYER SARAH MICHELLE GELLAR.
CAN I STILL DO EVERYTHING I WANT TO DO?
IF YOUR BEND GETS REALLY BAD THEN YOU MAY NOT BE ABLE TO RUN AROUND LIKE OTHER KIDS.
BUT THAT'S VERY RARE.
HERE, I'LL SHOW YOU....
SNAP
DISCO DANCE PARTY AT CERVICAL 7
I'M FEELING... FUNKY.
MY SUIT IS TOO SMALL!
CERVICAL 7 IS THE LOCAL FACET JOINT.. THE COOLEST JOINT IN TOWN!
MAN, I REALLY DIG THESE OUTFITS. I DIDN'T REALIZE MEDICS COULD WEAR SUCH COOL CLOTHES.
LOOK AT THAT GUY MOVE! MAN, I WISH I HAD SCOLIOSIS.
AS LONG AS I CAN DO WHAT I WANT TO DO, WHEN I WANT TO DO IT... SCOLIOSIS IS NOT A PROBLEM!
WHEN I GROW UP, I WANT TO BE THE BONE DOCTOR!

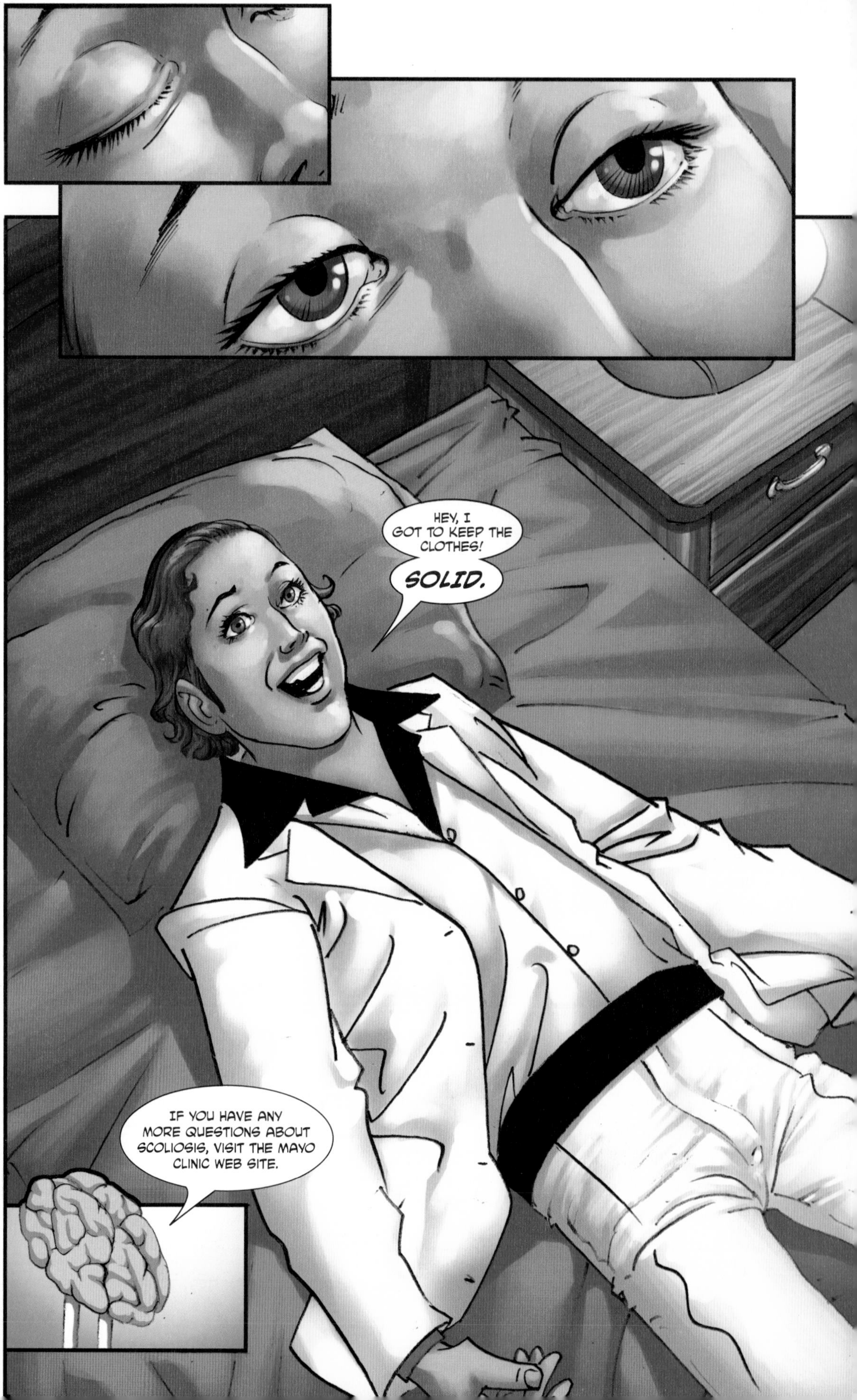
HEY, I GOT TO KEEP THE CLOTHES!
SOLID.
IF YOU HAVE ANY MORE QUESTIONS ABOUT SCOLIOSIS, VISIT THE MAYO CLINIC WEB SITE.

GLOSSARY

ANESTHETIC DRUG USED TO CREATE LOSS OF CONSCIOUSNESS
SO THAT PATIENTS CAN GO THROUGH SURGERY ASLEEP AND
WITHOUT PAIN.

BONES THE HARD INDIVIDUAL PIECES OF THE SKELETON, COM-
POSED MOSTLY OF CALCIUM.

BRACE A DEVICE THAT, WHEN FASTENED AROUND THE BODY,
PROVIDES SUPPORT TO THE SPINE.

CALCIUM A CHEMICAL ELEMENT THAT MAKES UP MANY PARTS OF
THE BODY, INCLUDING THE BONES AND TEETH.

CERVICAL REFERRING TO THE SEVEN BONES THAT MAKE UP
THE NECK.

COMPUTED TOMOGRAPHY (CT) SCAN A SCANNING TECHNIQUE
WHERE SEVERAL X-RAY BEAMS AND DETECTORS ROTATE
AROUND THE BODY, CREATING TWO-DIMENSIONAL CROSS-
SECTIONAL IMAGES.

DISCS FIBROUS STRUCTURES THAT LIE BETWEEN THE VERTE-
BRAE, HOLDING THEM TOGETHER AND ACTING AS SHOCK
ABSORBERS.

FACET JOINT SMALL JOINTS LOCATED BETWEEN AND BEHIND THE
VERTEBRAE THAT ALLOW FLEXIBILITY IN THE SPINE.

HEMIVERTEBRAE WEDGE-SHAPED VERTEBRAE THAT CAN CREATE
AN ANGLE IN THE SPINE. THIS CAN NARROW THE SPINAL CANAL
AND CREATE INSTABILITY.

LUMBAR REFERRING TO THE FIVE BONES THAT MAKE UP THE
LOWER BACK.

MAGNETIC RESONANCE IMAGING (MRI) A SCANNING TECHNIQUE
WHERE A POWERFUL MAGNETIC FIELD AND RADIO FREQUENCY
PULSES ARE USED TO CREATE DETAILED IMAGES OF THE
INSIDE OF THE BODY.

MUSCLE ELASTIC TISSUE THAT CONTRACTS TO ENABLE MOVE-
MENT WITHIN THE BODY.

SACRUM TRIANGULAR STRUCTURE AT THE BASE OF THE
SPINE, MADE OF NINE INDIVIDUAL BONES THAT ARE FUSED
TOGETHER.

SCOLIOSIS A MEDICAL CONDITION IN WHICH A PERSON'S SPINE IS
ABNORMALLY CURVED.

SCOPE A SMALL CAMERA THAT CAN BE INSERTED INTO THE
BODY TO ENABLE A SURGEON TO SEE MORE CLEARLY BUT
MAKE SMALLER INCISIONS.

SKELETON A RIGID FRAMEWORK MADE UP OF BONES, PROVID-
ING STRUCTURE TO THE BODY.

SKULL THE BONY STRUCTURE THAT PROTECTS THE BRAIN. IN A
HUMAN ADULT, IT IS MADE UP OF 22 INDIVIDUAL BONES.

SPINAL CORD A LONG BUNDLE OF NERVOUS TISSUE THAT
EXTENDS FROM THE BRAIN TO THE BASE OF THE SPINE AND
TRANSMITS NEURAL SIGNALS BETWEEN THE BRAIN AND THE
REST OF THE BODY.

SPINE THE COLUMN OF 24 VERTEBRAE THAT HOUSES THE
SPINAL CORD.

SURGERY A BRANCH OF MEDICINE WHEREIN PROCEDURES ARE
PERFORMED ON PATIENTS TO INVESTIGATE OR TREAT A
PATHOLOGICAL CONDITION OR HELP IMPROVE BODILY FUNC-
TION OR APPEARANCE.

THORACIC REFERRING TO THE NINE BONES THAT MAKE UP THE
MIDDLE OF THE SPINE.

VERTEBRA THE INDIVIDUAL BONES THAT MAKE UP THE SPINE.

X-RAY ELECTROMAGNETIC RADIATION USED TO CREATE IMAGES
OF THE INSIDE OF THE BODY.

FOR MORE INFORMATION

BAYLOR SCOLIOSIS CENTER
4708 ALLIANCE BOULEVARD, SUITE 810
PLANO, TX 75093
(972) 985-2797
WEB SITE: HTTP://WWW.THEBAYLORSCOLIOSISCENTER.COM
A CENTER THAT SPECIALIZES IN THE TREATMENT OF SCOLIOSIS.

NATIONAL LIBRARY OF MEDICINE
8600 ROCKVILLE PIKE
BETHESDA, MD 20894
(888) 346-3656
WEB SITE: HTTP://WWW.NLM.NIH.GOV
THE WORLD'S LARGEST MEDICAL LIBRARY.

NORTH AMERICAN SPINE SOCIETY
7075 VETERANS BOULEVARD
BURR RIDGE, IL 60527
(630) 230-3600
WEB SITE: HTTP://WWW.SPINE.ORG
ORGANIZATION DEDICATED TO FOSTERING QUALITY
    SPINAL CARE.

SCOLIOSIS ASSOCIATION (UK)
4 IVEBURY COURT
323-327 LATIMER ROAD
LONDON
W10 6RA
WEB SITE: HTTP://WWW.SAUK.ORG.UK
AN INDEPENDENT SUPPORT GROUP FOR SCOLIOSIS IN THE UK.

SCOLIOSIS ASSOCIATION, INC.
P.O. BOX 811705
BOCA RATON, FL 33481
(800) 800-0669
WEB SITE: HTTP://WWW.SCOLIOSIS-ASSOC.ORG
NONPROFIT ORGANIZATION FOUNDED BY SCOLIOSIS PATIENTS
    AND THEIR FAMILIES, WITH THE PRIMARY GOAL OF EDUCATING
    THE PUBLIC ABOUT SPINAL DEVIATIONS.

SCOLIOSIS RESEARCH SOCIETY
555 EAST WELLS STREET, SUITE 1100
MILWAUKEE, WI 53202
(414) 289-9107

WEB SITE: HTTP://WWW.SRS.ORG
AN INTERNATIONAL SOCIETY OF DOCTORS AND RESEARCHERS
   INVOLVED IN RESEARCH AND TREATMENT OF SPINAL
   DEFORMITIES.

U.S. DEPARTMENT OF HEALTH AND HUMAN SERVICES
200 INDEPENDENCE AVENUE SW
WASHINGTON, DC 20201
(202) 619-0257
WEB SITE: HTTP://WWW.HHS.GOV
THE GOVERNMENT AGENCY FOR PROTECTING THE HEALTH OF
   AMERICANS.

WEB SITES

DUE TO THE CHANGING NATURE OF INTERNET LINKS, ROSEN
PUBLISHING HAS DEVELOPED AN ONLINE LIST OF WEB SITES
RELATED TO THE SUBJECT OF THIS BOOK. THIS SITE IS UPDATED
REGULARLY. PLEASE USE THIS LINK TO ACCESS THE LIST:

HTTP://WWW.ROSENLINKS.COM/MED/SCOL

FOR FURTHER READING

ABBOUD, JOSEPH A., M.D. AND SOO KIM ABBOUD. *NO MORE JOINT PAIN*. NEW HAVEN, CT: YALE UNIVERSITY PRESS, 2008.

BLUME, JUDY. *DEENIE*. NEW YORK, NY: ATHENEUM, 1993.

FARNDON, JOHN. *HUMAN BODY: THE ULTIMATE GUIDE TO HOW THE BODY WORKS*. SAN DIEGO, CA: SILVER DOLPHIN, 2006.

FISCHGRUND STANTON, ANDRA. *PILATES FOR FRAGILE BACKS: RECOVERING STRENGTH AND FLEXIBILITY AFTER SURGERY, INJURY, OR OTHER BACK PROBLEMS*. OAKLAND, CA: NEW HARBINGER, 2006.

LAMANTIA, MARC, M.D., AND GARY DEUTCHMAN, M.D. *THE SCOLIOSIS DESK REFERENCE, A PRACTICAL GUIDE FOR IDENTIFYING THE EARLY SIGNS OF SCOLIOSIS*. NEW YORK, NY: SCOLIOSIS CARE FOUNDATION, 2007.

NEUWIRTH, MICHAEL, AND KEVIN OSBORN. *THE SCOLIOSIS SOURCEBOOK*. NEW YORK, NY: MCGRAW-HILL, 2001.

PARKER, STEVE. *SKELETON*. NEW YORK, NY: DK, 2004.

WOLPERT, DAVID K. *SCOLIOSIS SURGERY: THE DEFINITIVE PATIENT'S REFERENCE*. AUSTIN, TX: SWORDFISH COMMUNICATIONS, 2006.

WOOD, ELAINE, AND PAMELA WALKER. *UNDERSTANDING THE HUMAN BODY: THE SKELETAL AND MUSCULAR SYSTEM*. CHICAGO, IL: LUCENT, 2003.

INDEX

ABOUT THE AUTHORS

DR. KIM CHILMAN-BLAIR IS A MEDICAL DOCTOR WITH TEN YEARS' EXPERIENCE OF MEDICAL WRITING, AND A PASSION FOR PROVIDING MEDICAL INFORMATION THAT MAKES CHILDREN WANT TO LEARN.

JOHN TADDEO, FORMALLY OF MARVEL ENTERTAINMENT, IS A CELEBRATED COMIC BOOK WRITER AND DIRECTOR OF TWO AWARD-WINNING ANIMATED SHORTS.